Legal Procurement Handbook

Published by the Buying Legal Council

Edited by Dr. Silvia Hodges Silverstein

www.buyinglegal.com
2015

Published by Buying Legal Council
www.buyinglegal.com

First published in 2015

Publisher's Note
This publication is designed to provide accurate and authoritative information in regard to the subject matter covered. It is sold with the understanding that the publisher is not engaged in rendering legal, accounting or other professional services. If you require legal advice or other expert assistance, you should seek the services of a competent professional.

ISBN: 978-0692371640

Printed in the United States of America.

Cover design by Roswitha Büchting, Dessau Design, Potsdam (Germany)
www.dessaudesign.com

Dedicated to MJS.

Efficiency is doing better what is already being done.
-Peter F. Drucker

About the Buying Legal Council

The Buying Legal Council supports procurement and operations professionals tasked with sourcing legal services and managing legal services supplier relationships with advocacy, networking, research, and information.

- It is the voice of the profession and promotes the interests of legal procurement and operations professionals.
- It serves as a catalyst in bringing together specialists from all industries and geographies buying legal services.
- It supports legal procurement and operations professionals through advocacy, networking, research, and information dissemination.
- It advocates for the professionals and promotes the value of legal procurement and operations.
- It keeps members on top of legal market trends and legal procurement and operations best practices.

Our mission is to advance the field of legal procurement and operations, enhance the value and performance of legal procurement and operations practitioners and their organizations, share intelligence on sourcing legal services and managing supplier relationships, and document and promote best practices.

We identify and provide solutions to both strategic and operational challenges our members face and prepare them for tomorrow's opportunities and challenges. The Buying Legal Council facilitates an innovative dialogue between buyers and sellers of legal services, as well as other stakeholders in the legal market.

Please visit www.buyinglegal.com
Follow us on Twitter: @buyinglegal

Table of contents

Abbreviations...14

Introduction..15

What the articles are about 16

Deliver value through Legal Lean Sigma & project management.........22
| Catherine Alman MacDonagh

Research report: How clients buy corporate legal services 28
| Dr. George Beaton, Eric Chin, Daria Radchenko

An alternative to discounts 37
| Toby Brown

Creating a level playing field 43
| Richard Burcher

Bidding to win: Step by step...49
| David Clark

CEOs love procurement: How to deal with the consequences 55
| Timothy B. Corcoran

Tools for measuring AFAs...62
| Vincent Cordo, Jr.

Bidding to win: Six winning moves 68
| John de Forte

What's (much) better than a discount?..75
| Danny Ertel

A primer for sourcing LPO services...83
| Danny Ertel

Strategic versus tactical buyers..92
| Geraint Evans

How long does it take to make changes to this document? 98
| D. Casey Flaherty

Saving the "Trusted Advisor" relationship 102
| Charles H. Green

Procurement needs a new metric...108
| Charles H. Green, Bill Young

Research report: Legal & procurement in Germany............................114
| Markus Hartung, Arne Gärtner

How to win GSK's business 119
| Dr. Silvia Hodges Silverstein

Research report: The state of legal procurement..............................126
| Dr. Silvia Hodges Silverstein

"I bought the law" – Outside counsel management...........................133
| Lynn D. Krauss

What legal procurement really wants 140
| Andy Krebs

Research report: Bridging the gap between legal & procurement.......145
| Brian Lee

Procurement & pricing: The benefits of partnering...........................150
| Steven Manton

Procurement & outside counsel: The benefits of partnering 155
| Colleen F. Nihill

Achieving value through sensible collaboration 159
| Susan O'Brien

A primer on reducing outside counsel spend 163
| Susan O'Brien

Choosing preferred suppliers abroad 172
| Dr. Ute Rajathurai

Bidding to win: Before, during, and after the RFP process 179
| Melania Wenstrup

Successful legal sourcing..187
| Jason Winmill

About the authors... 193

The way in which legal services are bought in the 21st century is being transformed. The increased buying power and sophistication of clients and consumers in all market segments and geographies place a premium on understanding their motivation and decision-making. In some cases, the disconnection between lawyer and prospective client created by formalized procurement processes exacerbates the difficulties of pitching for new work. It is not that the age of the 'trusted adviser' is behind us, but the idea of selling time and seniority founded on longstanding personal relationships is certainly no longer the predominant model.

This new book offers a wealth of insights into how the buying and procurement process is conceived and managed, and therefore what might be more effective. No-one involved in buying or selling legal services can afford not to read it.

Professor Stephen Mayson
London, UK

"Procurement" may still be a four-letter word in the legal industry, but the legal landscape is clearly changing. And with it the recognition that it is incumbent upon the general counsel and her outside counsel to apply greater sourcing discipline to our profession to create competitive advantage for her respective corporate clients. As we began to accelerate our roll out of the DuPont Legal Model in the mid-90's, we were visited by more than a handful of sourcing or procurement department representatives of several large corporations. You could always sense as to whether the legal department had bought into these exchanges by their demeanor and posture during these sessions or whether they even attended the meetings at all. Few legal departments during this period embraced or even acknowledged the need for help from their fellow procurement professionals. But some did, based upon a "felt need" created by the general counsel's CEO. That was certainly not the way sustainable transformation occurs nor did it at the time.

So fast forward to the 21st century, the drumbeat continues for greater resourcefulness, process discipline and rigor as to how legal services are selected and priced. The external environment has changed but certainly not the perceived and real need for the legal industry to become far more cost sensitive and client focused. The other professional sectors have certainly had to do just that. As I have frequently reminded my colleagues both within DuPont and our network of providers, the only common metric among internal staff functions is their budgets and whether they met or exceeded them. So like it or not, we need to apply every conceivable strategy, methodology, and tool available to us to deliver value to our common client. And meet budget! It is like making a mortgage payment. You simply cannot afford to miss it.

So the publication could not have been better timed. The balance that needs to be struck with the procurement of legal services and all that flows from that decision is of critical importance to the representation, reputation, and risk profile of the company and how these services are priced and effectively managed. And like so many other challenges a corporation may face, collaboration among all of the parties—the business client, in-house attorney, sourcing professional and outside counsel—is needed to insure the optimum outcome. But in the end, the in-house attorney sits at all of the critical intersections and is, therefore, uniquely positioned to blend the sourcing discipline into the procurement process to insure that the company's interests are adequately protected and advanced. This publication provides invaluable perspective and guidance to whoever is involved in these decisions by way of case studies, checklists and opinion pieces. Hats off to Professor Silverstein for advancing the case for a far greater data-driven and disciplined approach to the procurement of legal services. The time has certainly come.

Tom Sager
Former General Counsel, DuPont Co.
Philadelphia, PA

Abbreviations

ABS	Alternative Business Structures
AFA	Alternative Fee Arrangement
CLE	Continued Legal Education
CPO	Chief Procurement Officer
FTE	Full-Time Equivalent
GC	General Counsel
GELRT	Global External Legal Relations Team
ITT	Invitation To Tender
KAM	Key Account Management
KPI	Key Performance Indicator
LEDES	Legal Electronic Data Exchange Standard
LPM	Legal Process Management
LPO	Legal Process Outsourcing
LTA	Legal Tech Audit
MI	Management Information
MSA	Master Service Agreement
MTR	Missing Time Report
NDA	Non-Disclosure Agreement
OCM	Outside Counsel Manual
PI	Process Improvement
PM	Project Management
PTW	Price-To-Win
RFI	Request For Information
RFP	Request For Proposal
SCI	Spend Control Index
SLA	Service Level Agreement
SQR	Savings/Quality/Reporting
T&C	Terms & Conditions
UTBMS	Uniform Task Based Management System

Introduction

Legal fees have become significant line items in many companies and continue to be under close scrutiny. Even as the economy improves, CEOs and CFOs see legal departments as cost centers that need efficient and effective management. They expect procurement will help drive down legal spend, improve accountability, prevent maverick spending, and deliver bottom line improvements. Procurement is tasked to support the company's core business strategic aims and obtain the best mix of quality, relationship, and value. Taking a process-driven sourcing approach, procurement aims to make the selection more objective and transparent.

Legal is still a challenging category for procurement. Procurement has to overcome accusations of interfering with the lawyer-client relationship, playing firms against each other to get the lowest price, and unreasonably squeezing firm's margins without understanding the effects on quality of advice. Procurement has to gain the trust of the legal department and demonstrate that their skills are useful to help pick the right firms for the right matters at the right price. Law firms have become accustomed to facing procurement. Firms that are prepared to be commercial, negotiate, and demonstrate value continue to win work at profitable levels from even the most demanding clients. Few today believe that an upward trend in the economy will result in legal services returning to being sourced by the legal department alone, without procurement.

The *Legal Procurement Handbook* contains the insight of experts working in and with legal procurement. It offers advice for those tasked with buying legal and provides guidance for law firms competing for work when procurement is involved. We believe that it will be a useful guide and companion for you and hope that you'll enjoy reading the articles.

Dr. Silvia Hodges Silverstein & Aria Antonopoulos, Buying Legal Council

What the articles are about

Deliver value through Legal Lean Sigma & project management
(Alman MacDonagh)

This article discusses tools like Lean Sigma, project management, and process improvement that help demonstrate a law firm's commitment to efficiency, quality, and continuous improvement.

Research report: How clients buy corporate legal service
(Beaton, Chin, Radchenko)

This article is based on longitudinal research on purchasing behavior of legal services in Australia. It illustrates what drives clients' perceptions and purchasing and encourages clients and law firms to design their respective purchasing/business development strategies in a manner that co-produces more value.

An alternative to discounts (Brown)
The author offers an alternative to focusing on discounts and hourly rates: careful scoping of matters. This approach will help legal and procurement to work together more effectively, resulting in better cost control and higher quality legal service to the client.

Creating a level playing field (Burcher)
This article offers advice for both law firms and procurement in today's competitive marketplace: it tells law firms how to deal with procurement's playbook and when to participate in an RFP for law firms. It also offers a list of do's and don'ts for procurement.

Bidding to win: Step by step (Clark)

Procurement has changed the way law firms need to market themselves and bid for business. This article leads law firms through the different stages of the bidding process and demonstrates that teamwork between outside counsel and the bid team is necessary to succeed.

CEOs love procurement: How to deal with the consequences (Corcoran)

Managing costs is a priority for all business leaders. When CEOs bring procurement in to manage cost, the author explains that it's critical to know procurement's scorecard metrics and understand the value the organization places on various legal services.

Tools for measuring AFAs (Cordo)

This article argues that AFAs need tools to measure the outcome, quality, and value of a matter or portfolio of matters. It offers different opportunities for law firms to improve the situation for both law firms and clients.

Bidding to win: Six winning moves (de Forte)

This article offers ways for law firms to successfully deal with the ever-increasing number of RFPs issued by procurement: from rigorous qualifying RFPs the firm should bid on, to developing a dialogue with procurement, to measuring ROI.

What's (much) better than a discount? (Ertel)

Negotiating rate discounts is a zero-sum game clients shouldn't play with their trusted advisors. This article offers ways to find value that does not come at the expense of outside counsel's margins: Effective portfolio pricing, joint matter management, and new delivery models. Such proactive collaboration takes time and effort, and should only be done with the right firms—which this article helps identify.

A primer for sourcing LPO services (Ertel)

Legal departments need to get better at budgeting and ensuring they get the right team for each matter. Procurement can help map legal spend and activities against a desired future state. This article gives insight into how procurement can help the legal department unbundle legal processes and successfully source legal process services.

Strategic versus tactical buyers (Evans)

Procurement's sophistication has great impact on law firms' experience when bidding for work and on the legal departments' peace of mind. This article compares the approaches of tactical and strategic procurement professionals and introduces category positioning frameworks as an instrument of strategic purchasing.

How long does it take to make changes to this document? (Flaherty)

Are my lawyers efficient? The author of this article wanted to be sure and developed a technology audit that would tell him whether outside counsel spent their time on value-added work or on wasteful manual labor that any basic, common software could do automatically, faster and (much) cheaper.

Saving the "Trusted Advisor" relationship (Green)

Lawyers traditionally see themselves as "Trusted Advisors" to their clients. This article discusses the benefits and risks of "Trusted Advisor" relationships between law firms and clients. It explains what to do when procurement's approach prevents such a mutually beneficially relationship.

Procurement needs a new metrics (Green, Young)

Procurement's role has changed, but the measurement and its focus on savings have stayed the same. The article explains that procurement needs a new key performance indicator, one that can be supported by internal audit and that aligns procurement with the interests of its internal clients.

Research report: Legal & procurement in Germany (Hartung, Gärtner)

Legal procurement has become a vital function to manage spend among Germany's largest companies. This article compares the findings from two research studies (conducted in 2012 and 2014) and concludes that procurement and legal operations need to collaborate and divide up the work to achieve cost cutting, reduction of complexity, and increased efficiency.

How to win GSK's business (Hodges Silverstein)

Winning business from big, prestigious clients like pharmaceutical giant GSK is rewarding, but the process may be daunting, particularly when procurement is involved. This article reveals how firms can do it successfully: Invest in your business side.

Research report: The state of legal procurement (Hodges Silverstein)

Legal procurement is here to stay and only continues to increase in influence. The findings from three studies on legal procurement give insight into their role, tools, influence, background, and approach. The article offers law firms advice on how they become more appealing to clients when procurement is involved in sourcing legal services.

"I bought the law" – Outside counsel management (Krauss)

Having worked both as in-house counsel and legal procurement officer— long before it became more common—the author combines her skills and knowledge to obtain cost-effective and valuable outside services. This article, an updated version of an article the author wrote in 1999, offers tactics for successful outside counsel supplier management.

What legal procurement really wants (Krebs)

This article explains what procurement professionals want, why they want to be involved in sourcing legal services, and how they can add value. It offers a list of do's and don'ts for RFPs and insight into procurement's (legal) supplier management approach.

Research report: Bridging the gap between legal & procurement (Lee)

Legal departments are often reluctant to collaborate with procurement because they value their relationships with outside counsel. This article offers a list of recommendations on how careful management of the legal/procurement relationship can result in great benefits for sourcing legal services.

Procurement & pricing: The benefits of partnering (Manton)

This article argues that a strong relationship between pricing professionals and procurement experts will be beneficial for both law firms and clients: financially astute and business-minded, these experts speak the same language and focus on efficiency and transparency.

Procurement & outside counsel: The benefits of partnering (Nihill)

This article shows how law firms and clients can benefit greatly from improved partnering during the different stages of the legal engagement, from risk assessment of a matter to negotiation, budget preparation, and relationship review.

Achieving value through sensible collaboration (O'Brien)

This case study discusses how procurement in a multinational company was able to successfully apply cost-cutting measures to an area of legal spend. It resulted in both real savings and the desired quality of advice. It also demonstrates the importance of a well-conducted search and selection of law firms and of tracking success.

A primer on reducing outside counsel spend (O'Brien)

This article suggests ways in which procurement can successfully approach the legal category and become trusted advisors to the legal department. It discusses basic practices that can make an impact on reducing outside counsel spend through engagement and billing guidelines, matter management and eBilling systems, competitive bidding, budgeting, and setting up AFAs.

Choosing preferred suppliers abroad (Rajathurai)

This article shows how a company selected its preferred suppliers in Japan. It guides the reader through the different stages of the process: from preparation, establishing and issuing the RFP, analysis of the firms' responses, the personal visit to the final decision-making.

Bidding to win: Before, during, and after the RFP process (Wenstrup)

This article shows how law firms can maximize their chances to win RFPs: From actions law firms can take before a company issues an RFP, during the RFP process, to after the RFP is over and the decision has been made.

Successful legal sourcing (Winmill)

Legal procurement varies widely in its approach, skills, focus, scope, impact, and results. For sourcing professionals, it is important to use available tools the right way, aware of common pitfalls. Sourcing can make progress in the legal category with a thoughtful and strategic approach and appropriate resources.

Deliver value through Legal Lean Sigma & project management

Catherine Alman MacDonagh

There is little point in being anything but blunt: firms that ignore Lean, Six Sigma, process improvement (PI), and project management (PM) do so at their own peril, particularly, when procurement is involved in the purchasing process. Clients can now determine whether a firm is serious. What is more compelling: a firm that tells them how efficient they are or one that shows them? There is an obvious difference between a response to an RFP with a cobbled-together paragraph of text about how efficient a firm is versus one that contains specific metrics, graphs, and process maps.

Firms that have embraced Lean Six Sigma early on are now able to tout their robust programs, and can point to cadres of Lean and Six Sigma practitioners, a host of project managers and a team that are skilled in both disciplines, and dozens of completed projects and millions of dollars in improvement benefits. They can speak the language of continuous improvement with their clients, many of whom have employed these methodologies for years and have cultures in which Lean Six Sigma play a central role.

Originally used by Motorola, Six Sigma's value has been proved in companies such as AlliedSignal, Sony, General Electric, Lockheed Martin, Boeing, Verizon and IBM, just to name a few. Lean was advanced by Toyota. Many corporations today eat, sleep and breathe continuous improvement. In addition to showing how they deliver value and manage work efficiently, law firms can change the conversations to identifying process improvements that benefit both the firm and the client—with no tradeoffs. By learning and speaking the language of process improvement, they can have discussions with procurement about the steps, variables, key deliverables and decision points that can be anticipated from various participants at all the different stages. To win and keep work, firms have to be able to make a compelling case that includes deep and ongoing continuous analysis of accurate and timely data and processes that employ the lowest cost resources who are capable of doing each task in a way that delivers exactly what the client wants, when and the way the client wants it.

Processes are the way law firms create and deliver value to their clients. Processes embody the knowledge of the law firm, department, practice group or team. Ideally, processes are our best practices. PI helps us determine the best way to carry out a certain kind of work to achieve efficiency, excellent quality of work and service, high probability of successful outcomes, and predictability. When we develop the capacity to improve processes, we can employ PM skills to select the best processes, tools, and skills to be able to carry out our ideal process every time. We also have a sense of how much effort it takes us to do and deliver a particular kind of work—information that is essential for pricing and where we can be more efficient. From the client's perspective, it is inconsistent to be told that a firm has decades of deep experience handling a particular kind of matter and then in the next breath have it explained that there is no possible way to predict how long something should take, the costs and impacts of what could happen at each step, and how much the whole project will cost. The combination of Lean and Six Sigma includes finding our own best practices:

- With **Lean**, we simplify processes, reduce the number of steps, maximize process speed, and greatly improve productivity. We focus on doing the right things by eliminating waste in processes.

- **Six Sigma** is focused on reducing and controlling variation to the extent that it is desirable to do so. We want to be just flexible enough but not so much that every time we start working on a matter it is a brand new adventure.

Put together, Lean Sigma is about deciding the best way to do something and then always doing those things correctly. The two disciplines are about addressing waste and doing the right things (Lean) and then doing those things right (Six Sigma). As such, when you employ Lean Sigma, you can differentiate yourself in the legal procurement process. Additionally, you will have metrics and results that you can communicate visually and show how things relate to each other.

Lean Sigma methodology starts by understanding what clients value about our activities. It delivers on the "client centered" promises that many firms make in their marketing and sales messages. It consists of investigating a process and improving it by using a set of five principles:

1. **Specify value in the eyes of the client.** We use the client's perspective to evaluate whether an activity is value-adding (activities that work to create a feature or attribute the client is willing to pay for) or non-value-adding (activities that take time and resources, but do not create additional value for the client). All

non-value-added activities are priority candidates for elimination or minimization.

2. **Reduce waste and variation.** We aim to minimize or eliminate waste (such as unnecessary, extra processing steps or non-value-adding activities). However, just because value isn't clear to the client doesn't necessary mean the step gets eliminated; it is an opportunity to have a discussion about why something is necessary, advisable or important to do from the lawyer's perspective. Even then, the client might not find the activity valuable but this is a greater reason to be highly efficient. In addition, we are also cognizant of the fact that processes are harder to operate and require more resources if they vary. Also, when processes vary, the results can be outside the client's acceptable range.

3. **Make value flow at the pull of the client.** When a process has "flow," the steps are linked so that we move from one value-adding activity directly to another, without stopping or waiting. There are no non-value-added steps, no waiting, and the process takes the shortest possible time from the beginning to the end. This short cycle time allows a law firm to be very responsive to the client. The idea of "pull" is that a law firm is able to create value directly in response to actual client demand.

4. **Align and empower employees.** To successfully and continuously improve processes, the firm must harness the power of integrated teams, able to leverage individual strengths to achieve extraordinary capacity for coordinated action.

5. **Continuously improve in pursuit of perfection.** If we do not continuously improve, we lose our ability to compete and function.

Those who have employed Lean and/or Six Sigma will attest that, as soon as they started to describe and measure a process, they began to see things that could be improved. Most of our processes fall far short of their potential and improving them will benefit both the client and the firm/department. Many RFPs today ask firms to describe their PI/PM programs. They are focused on understanding how the law firms are becoming more efficient and expect firms to provide recommendations as to how they can help the client. Without the language and tools of Lean and Six Sigma deployed on an institutional basis, this becomes increasingly difficult, particularly as the work, services, and number and depth of relationships grows between firm and client. Here are examples from actual RFPs:

- Please address how you will accomplish greater efficiencies. Do you employ project management techniques such as Six Sigma or Lean?

- How and why should [Company] have confidence that your firm will handle matters efficiently and in a cost-effective manner without sacrificing quality?

- What changes could [Company] implement to make your work for us more cost-efficient?

- [Company] seeks reliable, financially stable law firms that can meet stringent cost, quality, and service requirements. A team will evaluate each proposal based on various criteria, including, but not limited to... processes generating operational efficiencies.

Imagine you are discussing new litigation work with a prospective client. When asked about your document review process, can you claim to be operating at Five Sigma like one supplier of this service can? Do you even know what that means? Can you explain how and what you did to develop that level of accuracy? And are you able to state that you are performing

200 times better than the average in the legal industry today? Perhaps you have an opportunity to compete for work that involves a retail giant's portfolio of commercial real estate leases. Can you, like a competing firms is able to, tout that your firm has developed such a tightly standardized process that you have improved your response time from receipt of request to producing a draft of the lease to the same or next day? That you are able to be great project managers and continue to improve by capturing very detailed data about each transaction? That you have reduced overall time from receipt of request to execution of a lease from 168 days to 62 days? And that your speedy, reliable results have allowed other retail clients to open stores an average of 8 weeks earlier, which translates to tens of millions of dollars in increased revenue? Can you demonstrate to procurement that your approach has resulted in no tradeoffs, since your process allows the law firm to deliver this service quite profitably and reliably for a low fixed fee?

Firms are well advised to address the challenge of reconnecting value to costs for legal services, and determining the definition of value as defined by our clients through Lean Sigma. Many firms and legal departments have already experienced great success, both independently and by working collaboratively. It is a wise idea to get started before it is no longer an option, but a requirement by the purchasers of legal services.

Research report: How clients buy corporate legal services

Dr. George Beaton

Eric Chin

Daria Radchenko

Our large and longitudinal study in Australia focuses on what drives corporate buying behavior of legal services. It systemizes the intentions these clients have in respect of remaining with their firm, recommending the firm, complaining about the value they perceive, reducing the volume of instructions they provide, or exiting the relationship. The performance of law firms is measured on the following attributes or drivers of clients' buying behavior. Our analysis shows how weighted combinations of these drivers determine the criteria by which clients select firms and, once firms are appointed, how clients assess the service and the value received.

- Access to partners/ principals
- Access to international resources/expertise
- Caring about their clients
- Commerciality of advice
- Communicate effectively
- Price

- Cost consciousness (i.e. careful when spending on your behalf)
- Ease of doing business with
- Effectively managing conflicts of interest
- Friendly/strong rapport
- Innovation

- Problem solving capabilities
- Quality documentation (i.e. accurate, concise, easy to read)
- Reliability
- Responsiveness
- Technical expertise
- Understanding your business / industry

The drivers above explain the great majority of the variation we measure in clients' assessment of overall performance, value delivered, probability of repeat purchase, their propensity to recommend the firm, and the extent to which the client feels organizationally bonded to the firm. We have not yet measured how clients buy the services of so-called "NewLaw" firms, such as AdventBalance in Australia (which is similar to Axiom Law in the USA and UK), or LPOs. While they continue to grow in importance, samples are too small for measuring. Anecdotal evidence gathered from in-house lawyers suggests the weights of the drivers in their purchase decisions are similar to those applied to traditional law firms.

The procurement process at which we measure the attributes most important to clients starts with a list of firms the client would consider for a particular matter ('Consideration') and moves through to short-listing once the firms have been qualified ('Short listing') and then to final decision where a firm is appointed ('Final decision'). Once appointed, the incumbent firm is assessed on its performance and the value it delivers ('Assessment of performance and value'). Somewhere in the course of the relationship there are points where the client decides whether or not to recommend the firm to others ('Referral'), whether to continue to purchase and whether to purchase more services from the firm ('Loyalty'), whether to terminate the relationship ('Exit'), and whether to change provider ('Switch'). This procurement process can be seen as five critical steps taken by clients in selecting, using, assessing, and switching law firms:

1. Consideration
2. Short listing
3. Final decision
4. Assessment of performance and value
5. Referral or loyalty or exit or switch

While some of the decisions made during the purchasing process are formal, systematic and extended over a long period, e.g. adjudication of the appointments to a panel, others are informal and quick, e.g. a recommendation to a colleague whether to use a firm or an individual attorney or not. There is no evidence that the materiality of the criteria varies with the nature of the decision. Likewise, there is no evidence that the criteria at any stage differ depending on whether the client has a firm or an individual attorney from a particular firm in mind at the time of the decision. There are some differences in the weights that decision-maker in the client organization give to certain drivers; these are highlighted later.

Findings and Interpretation

Price is falling…and falling: Since the global financial crisis we observe the average price clients perceive continues to fall. Clients answered the question "How would you rate the fees charged by [Firm] over the last 12 months, where 0 = 'extremely low fees' and 10 = 'extremely high fees'?" In 2008, they were at 6.81, went up to 6.92 in 2009, and have been declining every year since then, down to 6.62 in 2014. The year-on-year change is statistically significant as the table below shows:

Year	Perception of fees charged on a 0 – 10 point scale
2008	6.81
2009	6.92
2010	6.80

2011	6.72
2012	6.69
2013	6.68
2014	6.62

Together with other evidence, it is indicative of an industry in the mature stage of its life cycle, growing only at the long run rate of the overall economy. This means that price becomes increasingly important for clients as they exercise their power in what is now a buyers' market.

Perceived price continues to be more important – but only slightly: Since 2003, we have measured the importance to clients of the drivers described above in considering which amongst several law firms ('Consideration') to appoint ('Final decision'). In our 2012 report we wrote "the largest change in the importance of price (in the final decision) occurred between studies done in 2008 and 2010". In 2010, despite a small increase in the importance of price and as negligible economic growth continued, price remained only the fifth most important factor in the final choice of provider.

These findings have not changed materially in the last two years, so in the current analysis we have examined the role of price in Consideration. Between 2010 and 2013 'Understanding your business/ industry' remained the #1 drivers each year. Price has become somewhat more important for clients in considering which firms to short list; rising from sixth position in 2010 to third in 2013. As a result, 'Leading expertise' falls from second to fifth position. When we analyze the proportion of the top five drivers as a percentage of all drivers of consideration, we observe this proportion is shrinking. We interpret this to be the result of the increasing sophistication of clients and the intensification of competition, as more firms are regarded as technically competent and suited to clients' work. This trend means finer and finer points of difference between firms will determine which are considered, and which are dropped. Finally and not unsurprisingly, we note that while cost consciousness ranks in the middle of the drivers of consideration, it becomes increasingly important as the final decision approaches, and in assessing the value delivered by an incumbent firm.

The importance of role and industry in affecting what's important to clients: Different decision-makers place different weights on the top drivers of consideration. GCs are typically more demanding than their C-suite counterparts. 'They want it all', placing more weight on 'Understanding your business/industry', 'Commerciality of advice', and 'Price' as the table below demonstrates:

Top three drivers of consideration	Percentage of respondents by roles who indicated the importance of each driver	
	Senior in-house legal buyers	C-suite buyers
Understanding your business / industry	32.3%	26.9%
Commerciality of advice	30.1%	21.9%
Price	23.7%	21.3%

The public sector considers 'Understanding your business/ industry' and 'Price' as most important, while private sector C-suite regards 'Commerciality of advice' as the most important driver of consideration as the results from our study shows:

Top three drivers of consideration	Percentage of respondents by sectors who indicated the importance of each driver	
	Government sector	Private sector
Understanding your business / industry	43.4%	24.7%
Commerciality of advice	10.7%	26.4%
Price	27.0%	17.9%

For law firms, this materially means the 'one-size fits all' and 'everything to everyone' approaches to attracting clients have been dethroned by our research. The key to attracting clients is differentiation by demonstrating a firm's domain knowledge in the key industries of its major clients.

Cost consciousness remains critical for clients: While price is important to clients when selecting a firm, our findings show it has little impact on clients' assessment of the performance and value delivered by firms once they are incumbents. How a law firm deals with fees as an incumbent is important, but it is not so much the fee level that is important. It is how the firm keeps the client informed about costs, helps the client decide what to brief externally, and how the firm deals with variations of scope and budget over-runs, that are crucial to clients' perceptions. These communication-related behaviors are what we measure as 'cost consciousness.' It measures the clients' understanding of and attitude towards the manner in which the law firm is spending their money. Cost consciousness remains the attribute with the equal largest impact on clients' perceptions of the performance of law firms they use as our survey results shows in the table below.

Drivers of performance and value in rank order	Percentage variation relative to all other drivers
Ease of doing business with	13.3%
Cost consciousness	13.2%
Caring about their clients	10.8%
Understanding your business / industry	9.9%
Technical expertise	9.1%
Commerciality of advice	8.7%
Reliability	8.1%
Friendly / strong rapport	6.4%
Quality documentation	5.7%
Innovation	4.9%
Responsiveness	3.9%
Communicate effectively	3.4%
Perception of fees	2.6%

Price again has not become substantially more important in satisfying and retaining clients. What influences client satisfaction and retention is how firms communicate and manage their costs. Firms that focus on cost consciousness instead of price reap rewards as their clients appreciate their performance and the value they deliver.

Every year when we show our findings to practicing lawyers we encounter the argument 'This is not how my clients behave; many persistently complain about fees.' In our view, these clients are simply negotiating—and practitioners are ill-equipped to respond. The easy answer is to discount one's fee—with the result that the client learns 'If I negotiate hard upfront or complain, then I will secure a discount.' Once clients have been conditioned to purchase on discounts, the profitability from the industry will continue to be eroded.

Why the more expensive firm is chosen: We also asked clients the question: 'Thinking about the last time you appointed a more expensive firm to provide legal services, what did that firm demonstrate that had the biggest impact on you choosing them?' The table below shows their answers.

Codified reasons for appointing a more expensive law firm	Percentage of mention in rank order
Leading expertise	25.9%
Understanding your business / industry	19.0%
Commerciality of advice	15.1%
Responsiveness	12.0%
Reliability	9.3%
Strong brand	9.0%
Quality documentation	8.7%
Access to partners / principals	8.7%
Ease of doing business with	6.6%
Excellent communication	5.6%
Friendly / strong rapport	3.7%
Innovation	3.0%
Cost consciousness	2.9%

Price	2.8%
Caring about their clients	2.6%
Other	4.5%

'Leading expertise' is by far the most important attribute. When leading expertise (25.9%) is added to the related attributes of 'Understanding your business/industry' (19%) and 'Commerciality of advice' (15.1%) it is clear that applied technical competence (summing to 60%) is three times more important than service ('Responsiveness' 12% plus 'Reliability' 9.3%) and 20 times more important than 'Price' at 2.8%. Equally importantly, price is positively related to clients' decisions. Price is a contributing factor in appointing a more expensive law firm. We conclude this to mean that price is a weak positive signal for quality. The heuristic role of price as a proxy for quality in intangible services and luxury goods is well known. Our studies confirm this applies in the legal services industry, too.

Further evidence of the small role of price in clients' buying behaviors is shown in our work on why clients switch from one firm to another. When clients who report changing from one firm to another in the last two years are asked why, about 5% say they were driven away from, or attracted to, the firm by price. A far greater proportion (24%) is attracted by the enthusiasm of the new firm and an equally large proportion is driven away because they are dissatisfied with the performance of the old firm. This is not to say that clients are not using their power to drive price down. But our findings support the view that this behavior of clients is tactical, not a fundamental shift in the materiality of what ultimately drives procurement decisions. The law firms themselves are leading a substantial portion of this price-down trend.

Evidence on discounting: In our most recent study, we asked clients about the discounts they had received. One-third of clients reported being aware of receiving a discount, with the average discount being about 10%. When it comes to big discounts, 20% or more, GCs tend to receive these much less frequently, 6.8%, than the C-suite buyers, 15.6%. The following table summarizes the findings by the respondents' roles to the question "What is the maximum discount on the hourly rate you have received from [Firm] in the last 12 months?'

Range of hourly rate discount received	Percentage of respondents by roles who indicated the level of discount received	
	Senior in-house legal buyers	C-suite buyers
Less than 5%	16.6%	16.9%
5% to less than 10%	34.4%	34.7%
10% to less than 20%	42.1%	32.8%
20% or more	6.8%	15.6%

Conclusions

Our research demonstrates what drives clients' perceptions and procurement behaviors towards a more sustainable and value-creating approach. Clients and law firms should draw design their strategies informed by the evidence in a manner that 'co-produces' more value. While there will always be tension in price negotiations, the recognition of what really drives the procurement of legal services will benefit both sides in the long run.

About the methodology: The study is based on annual responses of 3,000-4,000 buyers and users of legal services. The respondents are in-house lawyers, senior business managers, directors and/or owners of large companies and government agencies. The respondents are drawn from the clients of Australia's largest 35 corporate law firms and our analysis suggests it is representative of a cross-section of the Australian economy.

An alternative to discounts

Toby Brown

There is natural tension between legal and procurement. Their basic goals, on the surface, run in opposite directions. Legal is charged with reducing risk as much as possible, while procurement is charged with lowering the cost of reducing risk, which may increase risk. However, there are ways they can effectively work together; resulting in cost control and quality legal service to the client. Legal departments will need to add or designate resources in the group dedicated to the cost control effort and through that role engage with procurement. This new role will be the key to creating a truly productive relationship and driving the best results.

Many procurement efforts are started when companies reach a critical mass in size. They realize a centralized approach to managing their supplier relationships will save them money and ensure consistent input into their products and services. This input can be anything the company purchases, from copy paper to steel for bridges. Initially procurement has an easier go driving savings. Although it requires significant effort to find and combine supplier relationships, cost savings are readily obtained via purchasing power and utilizing a more methodical approach to negotiating contracts. After this initial benefit, procurement's role shifts towards a constant, diligence over cost control. It is charged with making sure that supplier contracts squeeze every dollar out of the administrative costs and cost of production for the company. Some companies in the retail space are well known for their prowess at this, as their margins are very thin and aggressive cost control is required to maintain a healthy bottom line. Such an aggressive approach can yield unintended consequences. In turn, this consequence demonstrates a need for balance in how far cost savings can be pushed. At any rate, the bottom-line for procurement is the bottom-line. And the way a procurement department shows value is demonstrating their impact on the bottom-line via cost savings; some to the point that their salaries and bonuses are driven by meeting such goals.

Legal's role: The role of the legal department was sheltered from procurement's cost savings efforts until only recently. Legal's job was holding down legal risks and taking aggressive action when risks were manifested into real problems—law suits. The annual budgets for these departments were not heavily scrutinized. Since the number of lawsuits and deals the company would have each year were unpredictable, the legal department made requests for resources as they needed them. Company leadership would approve, since failure to respond to a lawsuit could have significant negative financial impacts and deals had to be done. Not only since the Great Recession, things began to change, and cost savings found their way into the legal department. Around 2005, requests for discounts became more commonplace.

Since then, each year brought more and greater discount requests. When the recession hit, legal departments were already leaning in the cost control direction. In-house counsel were already feeling like the cost of outside counsel was too high, so they were onboard with addressing cost control. In some respects, in-house counsel had developed a level of distrust with outside counsel. But here's the thing—legal departments built the existing service and billing approach system in cooperation with outside counsel. They needed and relied on the dynamic that lead to high rates and billable hours. In fact, they were (and are) reliant on this system for their own internal talent. In-house groups hire trained lawyers from outside firms. Only occasionally do they hire people straight out of law school. We now have some dysfunction within the legal sphere, between former collaborators who are faced with a new, and not sure how to handle, problem.

Enter procurement: Around 2008, in-house legal departments started feeling more direct pressure to control costs. CEOs were effectively telling GCs that even with changing volumes of work, they would still need to control costs. In some circumstances, the CEOs introduced procurement to the legal department as a means for driving these cost savings. Often, procurement was thrust upon the legal department.

Early examples of procurement's involvement were likely not effective. RFPs from these efforts would ask odd questions, demonstrating a lack of understanding of how legal services functioned. For instance, one RFP provided a spreadsheet with types of services for each jurisdiction, broken down further into types of time keepers (e.g. partner, associate, etc.). The law firms' expected response was to input rates and number of hours per timekeeper type, per jurisdiction. Presumably, they were hoping responses would show competitive numbers on hours and rates. This all of course, assumed next year was going to be exactly like the current year. Not a good assumption. These early procurement-driven RFPs demonstrated the classic procurement method: unitize the product, then drive down cost per unit. This approach keeps the focus primarily on billing rates. This mindset appears to persist as many clients almost exclusively focus on billing rates as the metric for measuring cost savings on legal services. On one level, this makes sense. Lower rates should lead to lower costs. However, it overlooks many other important variables, including the number of hours worked. Before we address those other variables, we need to address two important points that arise from the focus on rates:

1. The focus is most often not on the actual rates, but instead on the percentage discount against law firms' standard rates. You can have competing firms with different rate structures bidding on work, but the apple-to-apples assessment of their bids is centered on the level of discount each firm proposes. Perhaps clients assume each firm's rates reflect varying degrees of expertise (and value) and therefore recognize and agree with the different levels. A firm with 10% higher rates reflects 10% greater value. Whatever the client's perception, this doesn't add up. The firm with higher rates might give a greater discount, but the actual rates paid would still be higher. The connection between lower rates equaling lower costs is broken. It is very hard to demonstrate cost savings with this type of a rate discount shopping approach. So why do clients continue to do this?

2. Because it is what clients know and can be easily accomplished. Asking for discounts is something clients had already done and firms agreed to them. So it was very easy to just ask for greater discounts. Procurement can be on board with this message, too. If last year the client had a 10% discount and this year they get 15%, savings should be realized. This is the message they can take to their leadership. "You asked legal to control costs. And we compiled by obtaining greater discounts from our outside counsel: Mission Accomplished."

So how can legal and procurement work together effectively and overcome the tensions? The majority of the market is still struggling with this and in many companies, procurement is still new to sourcing legal services.

Scope—the missing ingredient. The reason much of these cost efforts are struggling is due to a lack of focus at the fee level: How much does the matter cost? A big challenge is that the market has not traditionally priced legal services at that fee level. Both clients and law firms have little to no experience establishing fees as the known market pricing mechanism has been billing hourly rates since the 1960s. To establish fee-level pricing, budgets are needed at the matter level. To effectively develop these budgets, clients will need to establish scope for legal engagements. Establishing scope is something procurement can help legal do. For most product and service offerings, procurement likely requires scope of some type of specification of what is being purchased. Otherwise, they are not able to demonstrate cost savings. An apples-to-apples comparison is needed for that to happen. Since legal has not been developing scope for their engagements, procurement had to do what it could to establish those baseline numbers.

In a perfect world, legal should take the driver's seat in cost savings, with procurement acting as a navigator. By taking the lead role, legal will be in a position to drive results that include both cost savings and risk mitigation along with quality legal results. Legal departments that have been effective at controlling their spend have been those that take cost control head-on. The challenge is that most legal departments do not have the skills or personnel. Whereas law firms have been adding pricing directors, legal departments need to start employing similar roles. Cost control needs to be a primary part of their job description. With this role in place, legal will be better positioned to take advantage of the resources of procurement. The role can lead data-driven approaches that include budgets for matters above a predefined threshold. The budgets should include scope, such that changing situations can be addressed. Procurement will be in a better position to drive legal's cost control goals and become an important asset, helping legal understand its spend and track it in a much smarter fashion.

Creating a level playing field

Richard Burcher

More and more law firms have acquired additional pricing and price negotiation skills or brought in external pricing professionals to participate in the negotiation process. They have also become considerably more rigorous about whether to throw their hat in the ring on new client 'opportunities.' Triaging of invitations to tender or opportunities to pitch for work is critiqued more robustly and systematically than before. This is just as well because the direct and indirect cost of the firm's participation in pitches and tenders can be astronomical in the aggregate. To create something approximating a level playing field, I have suggestions for both law firms and legal procurement:

For law firms

The first thing law firms need to understand is that pricing involves a negotiation, and negotiation is a skill. If you are no good at it, you are going to be beaten into submission by your better prepared, more confident, more skilled and better resourced opponent every time. Most lawyers are good negotiators, except when it comes to their own fee where they often struggle. Those who have been prepared to do this have experienced greater success. Still, many lawyers find themselves powerless to deal with procurement's standard playbook, often consisting of one or more (sometimes all) of the following:

- Representations that all bids will be considered when the successful bidder has already been decided
- Indiscriminate, arbitrary and capricious inclusion of lop-sided contract terms to see which ones stick
- Representing that an agreement is concluded only to reopen negotiations in an effort to extract even better terms
- "Nibbling," resulting in scope creep for which there is a flat refusal to pay
- Changing the terms and deadlines of a price negotiation to unbalance the other side
- Refusing to provide adequate detail upon which to base an informed bid
- "My way or the highway" statements intended to convey indifference as to whether you or another firm gets the work.

Firms also often have to deal with various dynamics: Procurement tends to have different drivers and motivations to independent procurement companies and in-house legal teams and GCs are different again. When receiving an invitation to tender, firms are advised to triage and qualify those bids and pitches in which they should invest resources:

- What is the process for evaluating firms and their proposals?
- What are the names and positions of everyone involved in the process?
- Who is the ultimate decision maker and will we have any opportunity to interact with them or is someone else running interference?

- How many bidders are being considered and who are they?
- How many firms does the client wish to end up with?
- What are the selection and evaluation criteria?
- When and how do we get an opportunity to understand how we can add more value to the relationship?
- If you have no existing relationship with the client, why are you being asked to bid?

Beware of bid information memos where the in-house team or procurement flatly refuses to provide answers to even the most reasonable questions. That is disingenuous and quite possibly intended to deceive and confuse. It often signals another agenda. My advice: run a mile and let someone else 'win' the work. Once you have a good understanding of what you are up against, it is time to get to work on preparing your strategy so that the negotiations are just that, a negotiation, and not an unconditional surrender.

For procurement

One of your key responsibilities is to procure legal services in a way that delivers the best value and the best outcomes for your employer. No one can really take serious issue with this. However, the way in which many execute this objective leaves something to be desired. The following suggestions and comments are intended to be constructive rather than critical. I don't pretend that the list is exhaustive but I would characterize these items as individually and collectively a significant impediment to the advancement of the relationship and the kind of outcomes that you and your organization are probably looking for:

- **Engage & collaborate:** Coming at the task from the perspective that this is a zero-sum game will rarely produce optimal results for anyone. The most innovative, enduring and mutually fruitful relationships are ones that are characterized by a high degree of mutual trust, empathy, dialogue, collaboration and a general 'let's-make-this-work' attitude.

- **Stop running interference:** The legal category is a relationship business. You may feel that you are exerting your influence, control and importance by running interference between the primary relationship manager in the law firm and the project sponsor on your side of the equation, but all you are doing is presenting yourself as part of the problem, not part of the solution. By all means, participate in the process and act as a facilitator as much as an advocate for your organization.

- **Allow time:** If you present firms with completely unrealistic timeframes within which to respond, the quality of what you are going to receive in return will be commensurate. If you want a well thought-through, considered and interesting response, then you have to allow a reasonable amount of time for firms to produce these. If you are either disorganized and ask for it at the last minute or your belated request is cynically calculated to wrong-foot law firms by giving them little time to think about it, you are going to receive rubbish—little more than a rate card with glossy cut and pasted hyperbole and rhetoric about the firm.

- **Avoid conflicts of interest:** Unfortunately, too many procurement people confuse and conflate their individual interests with those of the organization they work for. This can manifest itself in such bizarre behavior as issuing an RFP that asks what the discount on headline hourly rates will be without actually asking what the hourly rates are. That sends a very clear signal that you really don't care about procuring legal services in a way that delivers the best value and the best outcomes for your organization. It is all about you presenting a 'scalp' to your paymasters and does nothing to assist the cause. And while on the subject of conflicts of interest, procurement people often bemoan the fact that the time billing regime incentivizes inefficiency. Quite true, but I'm far from convinced that procurement remuneration structures based on savings alone is any different, or that such incentives will do anything other than ultimately expose the organization to undue risk as a result of poor 'cheap' legal advice.

- **Provide as much information as possible:** The quality of what you get from firms and the specificity of particular proposals is in direct proportion to the amount of information that you provide at the outset. While some procurement professionals go to considerable lengths to do this, others don't. There is no doubt that putting together a quality RFP takes time and effort. However, that time and effort will be rewarded in the quality of the proposals you receive.

- **Don't use firms as stalking horses:** Firms are becoming increasingly sophisticated in their market research and triaging processes. Like the boy who cried 'Wolf', you will be found out. The result will be an ever-diminishing pool of quality law firms who elect not to be bothered dealing with you or responding to your invitations because you can't be trusted.

- **Be responsible:** You may be well aware of the fact that you are viewed as a trophy client. That does not mean it is either necessary or desirable to take advantage of everyone. It is not good for business relationships in the long run and it is not even good for business.

- **Don't ask for pricing innovation unless you mean it:** Generic and banal requests for "anything else you think we might be interested in" or "your proposals for alternative billing arrangements" have become commonplace in RFPs. It takes a lot of time, thought, care and skill for a law firm to put together really interesting and innovative pricing proposals. It is hence a complete waste of their time, resources and money to do so unless you are going to take such proposals seriously and you genuinely have the time and ability to evaluate them on their merits. Otherwise, save yourself and the firm the time and bother.

- **Put your own house in order:** Clients are often a significant reason for costs being higher than they might be. This can be the result of the organization's own inefficiencies and ineffective communication channels, a lack of centralized contact with the firm resulting in conflicting or confused instructions, and a propensity to get the law firm involved at the last minute which means that things are often unnecessarily conducted in a blind panic. It is worth taking time to have a look at the mechanics of the way that you engage with your firms.

- **Invest in professional development:** Chances are that you don't know as much about the pricing of legal services as you think you do. Pricing is a complex amalgam of traditional disciplines including cost accounting, statistical analysis, micro economics, behavioral economics, psychology, project management to name a few. The last few years have seen the elevation in status of pricing as a discipline, which, although 'old hat' in many industries, has only recently begun to be seriously embraced in the professions. You will need to invest heavily in constant professional development.

Bidding to win: Step by step

David Clark

Companies in the UK have changed the way they buy legal services. To gain the coveted panel appointments law firms recognize that a team of lawyers and business development can deliver a better bid than any separate part on its own. This collaborative approach provides reassurance to your clients that yours is a sophisticated, mature business that will deliver on its promises.

Large banks and insurance companies have increasingly shifted away from the 'Old Boy's network' of instructing law firms. As their organizations have become more regulated and increasingly more global and their discretion in buying legal services has come under greater scrutiny, effective security, policies, and business continuity are now regarded as essential requirements. Having agreed contracts in place, supported by service level agreements (SLAs) with measurable key performance indicators (KPIs) means the buyer will benchmark 'good' supplier behavior using meaningful service delivery criteria. To meet these requirements, panel appointments are common, with a number of suppliers (law firms or other service providers) engaged to manage a specific proportion of the annual volume of instructions.

At the outset, buyers often put in place a multi-stage process, requiring suppliers to provide responses to each stage. Many tender exercises are now hosted by the buyer or their appointed third party on a secure extranet or 'portal.' There can be anything from a single stage to three or four. Each stage comprises a number of questions to assess the 'bidders.' These questions can run into the hundreds. After each stage a shortlist of bidders is drawn up of those who perform best on a rigid scoring system. Where multiple stages are used, Stage One will encompass general business processes. The buyer will be looking for bidders who have been trading successfully in recent years, have appropriate policies and processes in place, hold the required insurance and have robust business contingency procedures.

This stage is all about ensuring that if something goes wrong, the level of exposure to risk is mitigated. This stage is often measured by procurement according to pass or fail criteria. Stage Two usually moves into expertise and experience in delivering a similar service to peer organizations. CVs, case studies, team organization charts, proof of capacity to deliver, statistics of previous performance, and the methods in place to deliver an effective service are normally required. Also indicative and competitive fees are often asked for at this stage. While there will be scoring criteria, these are often relatively fluid and subjective. Sometimes stages One and Two are merged, with the beginning being about risk mitigation and the end covering capability.

The traditional 'Final Stage' in many procurement exercises is the presentation or 'pitch.' The client's buying team, comprising procurement and the head of legal, will want to meet the relationship partner and some of the delivery team, including junior legal staff. At this stage, it is a matter of seeing if the parties can work together, whether the claimed level of expertise does exist, confirming that certain promises made in the submitted documents are realistic, and negotiating commercial terms. When pitching for panels or where the buyer buys on behalf of a collective of organizations, there may not be a 'pitch.' The chemistry here is less important to the buyer (usually a procurement person) and the bid is awarded from paper. This makes the construction of a compelling bid even more important. A final addition to the process is increasingly seen: a discrete and tough pricing negotiation after the bidders have proven they can deliver the service.

Now it is all about price. Many buyers at second stage will have drawn up their shortlists based to some extent on a price window—the range of fees they consider acceptable. Bidders deemed too expensive will have been weeded out. At this new stage, the buyer often provides more detailed criteria for the bidder to price against (perhaps based upon historical volume of instructions). This stage can be a reverse online auction.

A new term in RFPs is "reciprocity." This is where the buyer is looking for business opportunities which the law firm can introduce. Successful law firms offer such 'added value' through invitations to networking events, joint networking events, opportunities to joint bid, and introductions to contacts in a given market. What's new is that some buyers demand them.

Change on the law firm side. Procurement's shift of methods has resulted in a change on the supplier side: Bid teams are employed to co-ordinate and project-manage formal RFPs. Relationships are still key—they bring in the initial invitations to tender—and partners are still urged to 'get about,' meet clients, and network. This may also help position a firm effectively in the run-up to an RFP; their ideas may even be incorporated into the RFP and increase the firm's chances of winning. Close collaboration with the business development team is important to anticipate RFPs and ensure people are available when needed and undertake required pre-emptive work. This is especially important when the firm already works with the client. What are the buyer's thoughts of the supplier: what do they like? What can the firm do better? This gives the bid team as much 'ammunition' as possible for the bid.

Once the RFP is received, the countdown begins. The time given to respond to each stage of a tender continues to shorten. It is not uncommon for a bidder to have less than two weeks to respond, even over holiday periods. Here the project management skills of the bid manager come to the fore: Who is responsible for each part of the response? What information is already held? What additional information is required? Who is the owner of that information? What is the buyer truly looking for? In an ideal world all such questions will have been asked before and the bidder will have at least outline responses at the touch of a button. However, even if the questions are similar, chances are that the buyer's specific needs will differ. This is especially true for the second, more subjective stage of the process. It is hence imperative that the legal teams have a good knowledge of the pressures the buyer faces and their reasons for instigating a tender.

The bidder often operates a 'virtual bid team' composed of members of the legal teams who will deliver the service—across a variety of offices or time zones—as well as business support areas (HR, finance, IT, regulatory, facilities, information services, learning & development) organized around a lead partner and a bid manager. The lead partner has overall responsibility within the firm for the successful delivery of the bid. The bid manager is the project manager who is required to collate and manage all of the elements of the bid to ensure it is delivered in good condition, on time. A process is required reflecting the bidding organization's complexity, the level of detail the RFP requires, and the timescales for delivery. Everyone within the virtual bid team has to work together to deliver an effective bid within a short time while also carrying out their principal day job. At this point members of the legal team may feel exposed: This process is still evolving and buyers may only bid/re-bid once every three to five years; the lead partner may never have gone through this before; there may even be a feeling of a lack of control. Most professions train their practitioners to be in control and this lack of comfort will affect each individual differently. A key part of the bid manager's role is to provide reassurance to legal team members that their bid is progressing, to adopt a positive perspective at all times, and to assure them that the deadline will be met (and that they will win work!)—while ensuring that the teams provide the specific information required.

When the pieces of content are delivered to the bid team, they often have to be edited to fit the specific question, buyer, or tone of the bid. With online bids, editing often has to meet restrictive character counts. Many portals have a predetermined, locked upper maximum for each response. This means responses have to not only be in 'one voice,' but be succinct, engaging, and relevant. The skills required are not those required by a professional practitioner in their daily role and typically not held in equal measure by any one bid manager: some may be better project managers, some better copywriters, others creatives or authors, or analysts. This is why firms rely on team effort and the varied skill set held across the bid team.

Once a bid is won, it is time to begin collecting information, so that the firm is better prepared for the re-tender, even when that may be three or five years away. To do this, the legal team must work with business development to understand their performance through feedback and self-analysis. IT and finance can provide tailored financial content direct to the client and/or the legal team. This information should be treated like gold dust. It shows performance over time and provides the ability to monitor trends within the client and, when coupled with information provided by information services specialists, the wider market. This may be used to add value to the relationship and promote an incumbent towards becoming a 'trusted advisor,' which must be the ultimate goal.

CEOs love procurement: How to deal with the consequences

Timothy B. Corcoran

CEOs love to generate profits by reducing wasteful spending. They have grown fond of the procurement function because procurement helps reduce such wasteful spending. Yet despite the clear need for corporations to rein in spend and top management's mandate, the central procurement function tends to generate consternation in both sellers and buyers alike. There are few suppliers who leap with joy when learning that purchases will be managed by procurement and many buyers have a similar reaction when learning that their purchases must now be managed, or even just approved, by a procurement manager. What are the underlying sources of tension when it comes to procurement?

Waste and inefficiency doesn't manifest itself in the procurement of over-priced goods, so much as in undisciplined purchasing behavior that fails to generate economies of scale, or in purchases that foil standardization. A central procurement function also impedes purchasing influenced by self-enrichment, whether from the holiday ham to massive fraud.

Competitive cost advantage: The corporate tendency to maintain operating and purchasing independence effectively prevents the wider business from developing the maximum competitive cost advantage. Managing costs allows a firm to design, produce, and market a comparable product more efficiently than its competitors. In a price sensitive marketplace, of course, this "cost leadership" generates superior returns over competitors. Put another way, a business leader whose focus is limited to growing revenue is missing a clear opportunity to exploit cost control as a compelling strategic advantage. In economic downturns, business leaders in all segments who previously focused on growing top line revenue turn their attention to internal efficiencies and cost containment as a weapon in increasingly competitive and price elastic markets. All goods and services are subject to the economic principle of commoditization. In most sectors, there are a few providers whose reputation for excellence allow them to set prices with nary a concern that doing so will limit demand. Pragmatic and realistic business leaders know that very few truly occupy this space, and therefore there will be pricing pressure. Managing costs is an effective way to maintain margins, and often to improve margins, when clients eventually demand more for less.

Strategic sourcing or simply squeezing: The conventional view is that procurement operates merely as an administrative arm of the accounts payable department where it serves the purpose of finding the least expensive supplier for all commodities. And when like goods are differentiated only by price, the buyer gains leverage in a negotiation, squeezing suppliers of profits until the relationship is a one-sided affair. Sellers are often baffled and offended when a longtime client requires a detailed, 40-page response to an RFP before being allowed to continue rendering services, particularly when the prior work product has been deemed exceptional. The prospect of explaining the value of their unique services and taking direction on which factors the buyer now deems to be critical is daunting, particularly from buyers in procurement who have no domain expertise in the field.

The Institute for Supply Management asserts that its members must promote positive supplier and customer relationships while upholding one's fiduciary responsibilities and deliver value to one's employer, and do so without the appearance of unethical or compromising conduct. Spend enough time in business and you'll encounter a poor procurement manager, one whose focus is short-term cost savings and nothing else, who threatens cancellation or lawsuits, who tosses about the phrase, "the customer is always right" in a thinly-veiled effort to extort cost savings from unwilling suppliers. It may come as a surprise to learn that CEOs, even those who benefit financially from these tactics, don't want to be associated with such behavior. They recognize that any short-term financial gain is easily outweighed by the significant disruption costs imposed by constantly changing suppliers as well as the downstream impacts when a focus on quality control gives way to a lowest-cost mindset. Good procurement professionals have a healthy appreciation for the concept of total cost of ownership, which refers to related and adjacent costs, efforts, and time required to implement a solution. Selecting Product A because it has a lower sticker price than Product B is hardly a wise choice if Product A is incompatible with existing systems and therefore incurs significant customization to function effectively. Likewise, a project with a low estimated cost but delivered by a vendor with a terrible track record of staying on budget may be a worse bargain than the higher estimate from a vendor whose budgeting capabilities are precise.

The department of deducing differentiation: The role of effective procurement is to establish the necessary requirements, find suppliers capable of meeting the requirements, and select the supplier with the optimal balance of capabilities and cost. While this seems a reasonable task, the challenge lies not only with procurement managing this process, but with suppliers who are unwilling or unable to effectively describe, let alone quantify, their differential value. A seasoned procurement officer shared this typical exchange:

> Q. "Why do you charge more than your competitors for the same task?"
>
> A. "Because we're more capable than our competitors."
>
> Q. "How can you demonstrate that you're more capable than your competitors?"
>
> A. "Well, for one, we charge higher rates..."

Another veteran procurement officer faces this sort of absurdity regularly:

> Q. "Why should we hire your law firm?"
>
> A. "Because we've handled this type of issue hundreds of times."
>
> Q. "And what is your typical fee for handling this type of issue?"
>
> A. "I couldn't begin to tell you."
>
> Q. "You don't know what you've charged for this type of matter in the past?"
>
> A. "I'm sure I could find out what we've charged in the past, but this fact pattern is wholly different."
>
> Q. "If it's a wholly different matter, how will your experience benefit us?"
>
> A. "Because we've handled issues like this many times in the past."
>
> Q. "And yet you can't provide even an estimate of what the budget will be?"
>
> A. That's correct."

Price as a false signal for quality: A low price can be an indicator of efficiency, rather than a signal of low quality. In some industries, one competitor has a significant cost advantage over another and this can manifest itself in strategic pricing. This can be based on lower overhead or an extraordinarily efficient logistical supply chain. In the legal profession, law firms have yet to fully embrace the notion of competitive cost advantage. Most large law firms operate from prestigious downtown addresses with inefficient floor layouts that reinforce hierarchical organizational systems rather than maximize space utilization. The need for maintaining "bench strength" typically takes the form of expensive associates who can mobilize on short notice rather than a flexible work force, and this approach imposes high payroll carrying costs when these associates aren't fully utilized. There's a recent movement of back office operations to lower cost locations and law firms are beginning to embrace legal process outsourcing (LPO) as a strategic weapon.

Buying the safe brand: Every industry has its version of the adage, "No one was ever fired for hiring IBM." This means that hiring brand-name suppliers for a project provides protection from board and shareholder scrutiny even when the outcome of the project is not ideal. "After all," justifies the executive in charge, "If the best of the best couldn't save us, you can't pin the poor outcome on me." Those suppliers occupying the prestige brand space have greater pricing flexibility when others are challenged. This market position is the most elusive in any industry and is, by definition, reserved for a very small number of players. However, human nature and a belief in one's own marketing rhetoric convince many that their firm is one of the elite few suppliers in an industry.

Intangible differentiation: There's also an "X factor," a loosely defined set of skills, competencies, experiences, and relationships that form the basis for price differentiation for many suppliers. For some, strong relationships between suppliers and corporate executives have traditionally overcome price objections. In recent years, suppliers have discovered that their relationships are not as strong as they once believed: despite a long and solid relationship, a business executive will rarely choose an expensive supplier when the unjustifiable cost of doing so is likely to have a negative impact on his own compensation or job security.

For some, a deep understanding of the client's business can vault a supplier from "vendor" to "trusted advisor" status. This status is reserved for those who are proactive about offering insights and solutions before problems occur, who seek continuous improvement in the cost and effectiveness of their transactions, and who have an appreciation for the importance of budget predictability to corporate managers. The role of procurement is to demystify the X factor, to clearly identify which suppliers can meet the requirements of the task at hand, and, of these, which can do so at the most effective total cost of ownership.

Many suppliers who have lost a bid assume their competitors offered lower rates, even predatory unprofitable rates—when the bid is just as likely to have been awarded to a competing firm with higher published rates, but accompanied by a clear, well-designed project plan and budget. For procurement, the measurement of an effective selection of supplier doesn't start and end at the rate card price. A low-cost supplier that imposes transactional costs such as inefficiency, a steep learning curve, and endless scope creep generated by poor planning, is a poor choice. There are certainly procurement managers who select primarily on price—but it's the responsibility of the supplier to demonstrate differential value.

Take-aways: When dealing with procurement, it's critical to know the scorecard metrics and to know the value the business places on various legal services. Law firm leaders who focus on measurable differentiation through client focus, service posture, budget predictability, project management, and flexible fee arrangements are in a much better position to withstand short-term price pressures in today's competitive marketplace.

Tools for measuring AFAs

Vincent Cordo, Jr.

AFAs clearly continue to be on the rise as more and more law firms and clients adopt them. Rather than measuring input (in number of hours spent), AFAs focus on output and value. This necessitates establishing new metrics and KPIs that monitor the service level commitments and whether value is delivered throughout the matter life cycle and the entire portfolio. Developing a scorecard is useful to have all KPIs in one place.

General scorecard KPIs for clients and/or law firm include:

- **Cycle Time** Start to finish of tasks or matters.

- **Subjective Quality Grade** % or 1-10 grading on customer satisfaction.

- **Leverage** Average ratio between partner, associate, counsel, paralegal, other.

- **Net Margin %** Law firms measure potential profit; clients measure the potential margin on what they believe the matter is worth.

- **Net Savings %** Potential savings for the client based on historic information, previous work or bids.

- **Risk %** Clients and firms weight the potential business risk. Client examples: What are the calculated "quality" unknowns that can negatively impact the client by switching legal providers? How does switching providers save time, speed time to closure, maximize the value of time? Law firm examples: How much investment would be needed for working with a particular client and what is the long-term pay out? Is taking on this business in line with the firm's core strategy/strengths?

- **Legal exposure** Since the risk of legal liability varies greatly across industries and locales, firms need to identify the cost to the client and potential damage to their reputation.

- **Service Level Commitments** Clients measure if the firm responds to all client queries within x days of receipt, whether all financial reporting is regularly reviewed and the firm's invoices comply with the client's outside counsel manual.

- **Value Service (Investments)** How much does the firm invest in the relationship with the client? E.g., free general counsel support, large discount on a matter to try out the firm in another area, project management hours, tools provided or time saved for client?

- **Extranet tools** Ease of use and customization.

- **Reporting** Providing clients with real-time financial and task management information, and access to time entry (before billing).

- **Write-off** Time billed that a client sees as a non-chargeable line item with no value, or has a different view on what it should have cost, is written off from the bill. It can help track an attorney's efficiency.

- **Mark-down** Even though reduction in price means a decrease in margin for the firm, it can help increase utilization. E.g., time keepers that tend to have utilization cycles that dip for certain time periods until inventory starts back up, will benefit from more aggressive pricing during these dips. Mark-downs are often associated with margin degradation and profit loss, however that assumes the time keepers are at 100% capacity.

- **MTR (Missing Time Report)** Real-time reporting shows activities and trends prior to the bills being released (rather than time entry with a lag of a week to a month.)

Performance of the AFA itself should be measured by comparing budget, deliverables, budget management, reporting, and communications. Since priorities might shift over the course of a matter, indicators should be looked at in regular intervals and alert to which areas may need immediate attention. Metrics for AFAs include:

- Baseline and projected/actual costs for the total matter/portfolio
- Fiscal year-to-date earned value cost and schedule variances
- Cost trends
- Baseline and total task-based efficiency as measured by individual phase tasks
- Internal cost versus total legal operating cost
- Actual versus planned performance on internal recommendation (e.g. schedules, success milestones)
- Service level commitment performance
- Personnel experience utilization
- Systems and process levered

- Violations of outside counsel manual
- Corrective action management system performance
- Training statistics

Firms need to ensure that clients compare apples-to-apples. Comparing the services under an AFA of one firm with the services billed on an hourly basis by another firm makes little sense. Shadow billing is not enough and often counterproductive. Helping the client define units of measurement as a standard would help with grading on legal output, leaving less open to interpretation. Useful tools to do this include:

- **Task-Based Billing Performance:** Measuring actual performance and comparing received value to expected value/outcome.

- **Outside Counsel Manual (OCM):** Monitoring adherence to the OCM is critical to improve pricing, billing, and quality standardization.

- **Legal Process Management (LPM):** Applying a disciplined approach to budgeting and work plan development, and actively monitoring and managing each matter using real-time financial reporting.

Many clients and firms wonder how they can best implement a pricing system that helps gauge effort, investment (for both client and firm), successes, and reporting on quality. Ways to address this include:

Opportunity 1: Matter Staging is when the client's legal procurement team prices a matter based on what it would cost if the legal department was working on it. The client then sets up a matter budget/work plan, and tracks time against that matter in a task-based approach, and manages the matter the way any firm would be expected under the client's requirements. After completion of the matter, the legal team and procurement perform an action review, which gives the client an opportunity to scorecard and set quality standards on the matter, based on the KPIs agreed upon. Matter staging helps provide and capture historic detail for pricing and managing future matters. It also helps clients on internal budgeting and establishing pricing references, and can be used to compare firms in an unbiased fashion having removed some subjectivity. It's best to look at price and value on a portfolio basis rather than matter basis.

Opportunity 2: SQR (Savings/Quality/Reporting) Volume Distribution If a firm takes on a matter for a new client as a loss leader (in the hope to expand their volume with this client), the law firm is investing in the client relationship. It's then important that client and firm agree on what will be measured and how the client values the risk the firm is taking: Assess the authority level your procurement contact has in driving the business decision. Support them by presenting and defining units of measure metrics that can be levered, which will address business-level subjectivity. Build a strong link between your pricing/LPM team and the client's procurement/LPM experts to collaborate and keep track of KPI, financials, volume, and mark-down discounting. SQR helps when clients don't use AFAs or volume discounts that were agreed upon.

Opportunity 3: LPM Scorecard Even when an AFA is in place, most billing systems are set up to pay firms by the hour. If the system is configured to focus on driving cost, quality or value will be hard to gauge. It is hence better to bill AFA arrangements in percentages, such as 30% of the price billed in Q1, 40% in Q2, and the final 30% upon completion. Clients are well advised to create an LPM scorecard that firms must adhere to and are held accountable to. It contains budget templates with UTMBS codes and/or custom task codes, service level commitments, and KPIs. For example, it would map out a budget plan, track cost and leverage, and assigns task codes to each step so one can run reports on the health of a matter. It would list the UTBMS codes, the corresponding tasks, the partner in charge of the task, as well as total budget hours. For a transaction, each phase would have a fee total (e.g. F100 "Due Diligence" would include F110 "Draft List," F120 "Communication with Buyer," F130 "Communication with Sellers' Counsel" and so on). The budgets for all phase codes (F100-F600) would then add up to the total budget for the transaction.

Opportunity 4: Matter Profiling captures details of a matter at the onset and puts them into the tracking system. It allows having historic reference on billing arrangements, discounts, AFA language etc. This tool saves time when lawyers and staff look for matter details once the matter has started. It also allows quick pulling of information on how many cases are on an AFA basis, or which ones are in a certain practice group etc. Gathering profile information is essential for clients. It will provide more details around what matters should cost, trends, and how to track quality, moving away more and more from subjectivity being the primary driver.

Bidding to win: Six winning moves

John de Forte

Law firms have had to contend with an increase in the volume and complexity of tenders. Many have set up bid departments to help them cope. While this has strengthened their ability to respond, tendering continues to be an area where good practice often has to defer to constraints on time, budget, and resources. The six 'winning moves' help take bidding for new business onto a higher plane.

1. Qualify rigorously: You shouldn't waste resources on tenders you can't win or which are unsuitable. Focusing on the most appropriate opportunities is critical to achieving and maintaining a decent win rate. The tendency to chase too many targets varies from firm to firm, and often from department to department. General practice firms are more susceptible than niche operators, or others where the client base falls into clearly defined categories. Bid departments are redoubling their efforts to get their firms to be rigorous about the qualifying process. Lawyers don't always appreciate it. It's also difficult to formulate a clear policy and get people to stick to it. If the qualifying criteria are too vague, they will be easy to overlook; too rigid, and fee earners will say their entrepreneurial spirit is being stifled by bureaucracy. A flexible, but robust approach is to require prospective bidders to apply four tests before pressing on. Make fee-earners jump through these four hoops every time they want to submit a tender, and see the firm's win rate improve.

Strategic	Tactical
Core business?	Existing relationship?
Target sector?	Access during tender?
Target client?	Price competitiveness?
Logistical	**Commercial**
Resource availability-assignment?	Profitability?
Resource availability-tender?	Risks?
	Tender costs?

The strategic quadrant has as much to do with whether the firm genuinely wants the work, as whether it can win it. On closer inspection, the assignment may not fit into the firm's core business and won't advance its growth strategy. Perhaps it's a piece of work you wouldn't turn away if it landed on your doorstep. But that's a different proposition entirely.

A range of factors might influence your estimation of your chances of winning the bid. But none is likely to be as important as whether you have an existing relationship with the organization issuing the bid. If you don't have an existing relationship, at least ensure you will get access to the decision makers during the tender process. Otherwise, your chances of being successful are less than one per cent. Before going ahead, firms should know whether they are likely to be able to compete on price (see 'price-to-win', below). As for the logistical and commercial considerations—they need no further elaboration.

2. Develop a dialogue with procurement: The role of procurement is not confined to administering tender processes. Increasingly, procurement is involved in developing tools and metrics for assessing supplier performance and getting greater value from service providers. Firms which help the client to further these aims are putting themselves in a good position to win and retain work in the future. Once a tender is in progress, the scope to achieve this is limited. With key clients and targets, firms need to be developing and maintaining a relationship with procurement contacts over the longer term. Here is a potential role for senior business development people. Just as partners continue to nurture the relationship with the in-house legal team, business development is well placed to maintain contacts with procurement—who are in many respects their opposite numbers. The evolving relationship with procurement is important because firms are increasingly required to do more than provide expert legal advice: they are expected to contribute to the overall effectiveness and efficiency of the legal function. Responses to questions on added value in RFPs will be all the more persuasive if they reflect continuing dialogue with procurement about how external legal advisers can best support the business.

3. Embrace independent review: To achieve the best results, a greater degree of objectivity should be built into the process: It is good practice to appoint a partner experienced in bidding who is not part of the proposed team to act as a counselor. His or her role is to provide an authoritative and independent perspective on all key decisions, including the selection of the leader and other members of the service team, where to pitch the fees and whether to proceed with the bid in the first place. Presentation teams should rehearse in front of the counseling partner and others not involved in the tender. (That needs to be carefully orchestrated to avoid the undermining effects of negative or conflicting feedback.) Their primary role isn't to improve the presenters' delivery skills, but to ensure that the team comes across as a cohesive, unified unit—something which may be difficult for the team itself to judge. Independent input is also essential for debriefing at the end of the process. That is a critical part of measuring your return on tender activity (see point 6).

4. Create tailored propositions: Many law firm bids documents aren't 'proposals,' they're mini-brochures or credentials statements. Sometimes that is all that seems to be required or is possible. Yet GCs, CEOs, trustees, owner managers, and procurement officers expect the tenders to be tailored to the organization's particular requirements. Partners need to invest time in thinking through the issues affecting the client and develop a response which addresses them specifically. This requirement highlights the importance of having an existing relationship with the organization, or at least access to decision makers during the tender. This is necessary to develop a genuine understanding of the organizations' objectives, the expectations it has of its legal advisers, the issues and challenges it faces. Seldom does the RFP provide anything better than a superficial glimpse of these matters.

5. Adopt 'price-to win' methods: There's little sign that corporate buyers are willing to relax their pressure on fees as market conditions improve. Approaches to identify a level of pricing that is competitive have not changed fundamentally over the years. The team puts all the effort into developing a proposal that they hope will appeal to the decision makers. Usually with the deadline approaching, somebody will calculate how much it's going to cost to deliver the service; then a cabal of senior partners takes a view on the level of the profit that can be built in without scaring off the potential client.

As corporate budgets have continued to come under pressure, price has become the primary factor driving contract awards: across sectors, more than 80% are made to the lowest priced, acceptable bidder. A cost-driven marketplace demands that solutions are determined by a clear conception of what the winning price is going to be—not the other way round. Price-to-Win (PTW) is transforming the competitive landscape. Companies bidding for large contracts in the defense, IT, and outsourcing sectors have adopted PTW. It is increasingly used in professional services, including accounting firms and management consultancies. There is no reason why it can't be embraced by law firms. PTW involves in-depth competitor analysis, including pricing estimates based on competitors' past performance and likely approach to the solution.

A common technique is the appointment of a 'black hat' team to second-guess competitors' pricing strategy. Another critical element is setting work-streams a price target and incentivizing them to undershoot it. A further implication is that firms need to adjust the way they allocate bid resources. One suggestion is that they should spend at least 10% of the overall budget on competitor analysis and that strategic pricing should get a similar slice of the cake. All of this suggests that the 'pricing strategist' could become one of the more sought after business development specialists in the law firms of tomorrow.

6. Measure return on investment: Most firms keep a record of wins and losses. Useful as it is to know your conversion rate, it can't provide any real insights into which opportunities you should be pursuing or leaving alone, or the relative costs and benefits of bid activity. By measuring return on investment more accurately, firms can learn how best to deploy their resources. There are four dimensions to take into account for calculating ROI:

- Estimated contract value
- Opportunity cost
- Intangible benefits
- Overhead cost

The costs of preparing a tender can be quantified by the number of hours spent by fee-earners on the exercise, multiplied by hourly rates appropriately discounted to reflect current utilization levels. Add to this the contribution of the firm's bid department, expressed as an hourly rate based on overhead cost as well as any 'hard' costs—such as design and print or consultants' fees. The value of a winning tender can be treated as the estimated fee income that will accrue as a result of it over a one-year period. If the assignment is a recurring or long term appointment, this figure can be multiplied—although it is best to do so on a reasonably conservative basis.

Revenue gain, however, needs to be seen in a wider context. Where the firm is an incumbent panel member, for example, it may be appropriate to measure the success of the tender in terms of the increase or otherwise in the firm's likely share of client spend—rather than simply by registering whether the firm has retained its panel place. Similarly, it would be wrong to assume that if the firm is not appointed, the exercise has been of no value. Apart from possible training benefits (enabling partners and staff to gain experience and improve tendering skills), a good tender performance may put the firm in a stronger position to win work from the target organization in the future.

A systematic debriefing program is indispensable in gauging the less tangible benefits and is an integral part of measuring ROI. Some firms still under-invest in the process of getting feedback. Engaging with decision makers about the firm's tender performance is a form of high quality market research. If done properly, it will tell you a lot more than just why the firm won or lost. For major tenders, debriefs should be carried out regardless of the outcome of the tender. Wherever possible, they should be conducted face-to-face by an experienced interviewer who is unconnected to the proposed service team. By incorporating a quantitative element, the findings can be aggregated and used as part of the ROI analysis. This requires some yes/no questions among those designed to elicit more nuanced answers. The debrief interview might include the question: 'as a result of the tender, are you more or less likely to employ the firm in the future?' Over the longer term the answers can be tested by monitoring which tenders lead to new opportunities to bid for work or even directly to instructions, regardless of the apparent outcome at the time.

Any attempt to assess ROI must involve subjective assumptions about cost and value. Even an approximate estimate of the costs and benefits would help firms to ensure resources are used effectively. Which brings us back to where we began—the need for a rigorous qualification process to ensure that the firm's efforts are channeled into the most appropriate and realistic opportunities.

What's (much) better than a discount?

Danny Ertel

A couple of years ago, I suggested that GCs should "say no to discounts" and stop settling for short-term, often illusory, gains that come at significant cost to the relationship with their preferred outside counsel. I was only half-kidding at the time, and I think the argument is as strong today as it ever was: If you buy legal services on a billable hour basis and you control only the hourly rate, you risk ultimately not achieving material savings. The time and materials model depends on two inputs, price times quantity. As many legal departments have learned, unless you control both variables, you cannot say you have "legal spend under control." It's not a question of law firms fraudulently running up hours; it is recognizing how lawyers are trained and the common perception that our work "could always be a bit better" if we spent some more time improving the document. In the absence of clear expectations or controls about "what 'done' looks like" or the value of a set of activities, you should not expect significant efficiency improvements.

If you leave the basic price times quantity model in place, and rely on law firms having excess capacity to enable you to squeeze them on price, any savings you achieve will last only as long as that excess capacity persists. Even in the slow economic recovery we have experienced, law firm hourly rates have already started to go back up. Rate discounts may have set the clock back by a handful of annual increases, but they have not really changed the structure of how legal services are bought, sold, or delivered.

If you negotiate with outside counsel about how much they will discount their rates, it is very easy to damage the trusted advisor relationship. Whether or not you actually achieve any year-on-year savings, rest assured that outside counsel feel they have "lost" something when they cut their rates. Some of that is inherent to discounting, which leaves highly-trained professionals literally feeling devalued. But even more of it comes from the way discounts are negotiated: We invariably ask for a larger discount than we will ultimately accept, teaching our counterparts not to believe the first thing we say; and then we resist their attempts to bring us closer to their number, teaching them that to get a reasonable agreement they also have to exaggerate how difficult it is for them to make any further concessions. In the end, even when we reach agreement on a specific discount, we are left uncertain whether we actually got a good deal or whether we should have held out for more. And to some greater or lesser extent, we have put some dents and scratches into what should be a trusted advisor relationship.

Moreover, if you really want to convince a law firm to lower their rates, they have to believe that if they do not, they will lose your business. But unless you have a fairly disciplined counsel selection process, it may be difficult to make that threat seem credible. And even if you can easily move work away from some firms, that is not necessarily what you want to do or should do to get the services and quality you need. Negotiating with outside counsel on the basis of whether you are willing to use someone else or they are willing to walk away from the business unless you meet their rate demands is a terrible way to start work on a matter. Even as the economy recovers, chances are good that you still have some bargaining leverage with outside counsel. All the available evidence suggests that legal departments have enhanced their internal capabilities so they need to send out less work. There has also continued to be significant convergence, with legal departments consolidating their work with fewer law firms, and therefore becoming more significant clients of those firms.

The fact that the buyer makes significant use of the provider and that the provider relies on the buyer for a significant amount of revenue can be used either coercively (with the implicit threat to take work away from the provider unless they make some concessions) or it can be used collaboratively, making use of the greater opportunities to work together, build relationships, and become increasingly interdependent. It's not just a question of whether you are pleasant and polite as opposed to difficult and overbearing in your discussions about price. The difference between two very different ways to approach a more extensive relationship between a buyer and a service provider lies largely in whether you negotiate about the value you expect to obtain from the relationship or the margin you are willing to leave the provider. Negotiations about rate discounts treat value and margin as a zero-sum game. Any value gained by the legal department comes directly and entirely at the law firm's expense. Playing a zero-sum game with a trusted advisor whose role is to help in-house counsel manage legal and regulatory risk just seems plain foolish. Instead, legal departments and their preferred outside counsel should be exploring ways to:

Work collaboratively	so it's good for the relationship
to restructure	so the effects are lasting
how they work together, and	both the supply and the demand for services
the value proposition for the services provided.	to achieve the elusive "more with less."

AFAs, legal process outsourcing (LPO), and project management help achieve this. Technology can reduce the time required to carry out tasks or change who performs which tasks from where. There are many more choices today about how to structure legal work. The choices in-house counsel and their preferred external partners make will move the needle on legal costs, predictability, and value—or not. I have started seeing examples of counsel finding ways to improve the value proposition for the client, without taking every gain out of law firm's margins.

- **Effective portfolio pricing** gives clients greater predictability and the ability to plan. That is also highly desirable to law firms, who need to plan their own hiring, make investments, and rely on a particular cash flow. However, you don't get workable portfolio pricing without significant investment of time, by both sides, to understand the portfolio and agree on proper boundaries for what is included. It also requires a collaborative discussion on classifying matters and managing them for efficiency and effectiveness.

For example, working closely with their preferred outside counsel, the legal department of a large life sciences company analyzed several years of claims history and came up with a scheme for slotting cases into different price categories at matter opening. They paired that with a tiered volume structure to help the law firm manage the risk they were taking on. The legal department achieved some savings and gained the tools to engage different business units in discussions about the numbers of cases in each category and how to take that into account to develop budgets across the life cycles of their different products.

- **Joint matter management** enables legal departments to let outside counsel do what they do best, while providing the necessary level of oversight and engagement about how a matter will be handled. Law firms get the benefit of a more informed client, less likely to seek after-the-fact write-offs because they didn't like how a matter was staffed or were surprised by what it cost to get something done. Following the "4 Ps" of effective matter management adds the necessary structure: Start by developing a shared view of the client's priorities, the expected in-scope products, the process they will follow (to get the work done and to stay closely aligned), and the people who will be part of the effort.

  For example, a financial services institution found that by working through such a process jointly and collaboratively with outside counsel, they could get better results than by unilaterally imposing outside counsel guidelines and threatening not to pay bills that were non-compliant. Across a tangled (and costly) web of related matters, including state and federal investigations, claims by institutional customers, and investor class actions, they were able to go from a contentious, line-by-line review of every invoice into a forward-looking monthly planning effort, saving both inside and outside counsel a lot of time and aggravation.

- **Developing new delivery models** can solve real problems, improve law firms' bottom lines, and still save money for their clients. When clients articulate pain points and outside counsel thinks more broadly about how to solve those problems, interesting ideas come to fruition. Orrick's corporate secretarial services, developed originally for Cisco and then extended to other clients is an interesting example. Cisco's internal database for tracking subsidiaries, signing authorities, registration obligations, board resolutions, etc. was reaching the end of its useful life and was taking too much time and effort to maintain. Orrick rebuilt it on a more modern platform, standardized the work to be carried out by local counsel around the world, and turned it into a managed service at a significant annual savings. In doing so, they saved the client money and distraction, created a new profit center for themselves, and deepened their relationship with Cisco.

The key to finding value that does not come at the expense of outside counsel's margins seems to lie in posing a somewhat different question: Instead of asking "how do we get better rates from outside counsel?," a more useful mindset focuses on figuring out how to become a more attractive client. That does not only mean giving selected firms more work (additional work at lousy rates is still unprofitable) but becoming less expensive to serve. While some legal departments leverage their spend and their eBilling data to ensure they get the lowest rates, that does not necessarily make them the priority clients of those firms.

Getting outside counsel to bend over backwards for them, staff their best teams on their matters, and bring their best ideas to them without simply overpaying, that is the holy grail of outside counsel management. The proactive, collaborative exploration of the potential value opportunities in the relationship takes effort. But it is not worth making that investment in every outside counsel relationship. Some services can simply be performed by the lowest qualified bidder. To identify the right firms, ask yourself:

- Are you spending a significant amount of money with this firm? If the answer is no, chances are that it will be difficult to get their attention.

- Can you articulate some initial hypotheses of how you could change the way you consume legal services, or how outside counsel could change how they staff and perform the work that could add value to you or reduce their costs? This could be unbundling work and reallocating tasks to lower cost resources (at the law firm, the client, or a third party), making greater use of technology, or developing (and reusing) more standardized forms and templates.

- Can you imagine a different way to share the risks associated with how much work you will have for and how much time and effort any given matter will take? If not, you may not be trying very hard – there are different models for pricing professional services, including unit pricing, portfolio pricing, value-based pricing, volume commitments, etc. But effective risk sharing/risk spreading requires that the relationship be more than episodic.

- Could you effectively move more work to this firm if the value proposition improved? If the answer is no, then again, the exercise may not be worth your or their time, as many of the solutions you might come up with would require increasing the volume of work you do with them to realize real gains in efficiency.

If you answered yes to these questions, chances are good that you have a real opportunity to significantly improve the value equation: to make your legal spend go further and be more predictable, to gain greater visibility into what the real choices and levers are for managing legal costs, and to make your preferred outside counsel work hard to preserve your relationship because it is also highly valuable to them.

These collaboration efforts seem to work best when led by the client. Law firms have a harder time initiating true collaborative efforts to improve their clients' value propositions, without those efforts devolving into (or at least being perceived that way) cross-selling exercises. If the client structures the exercise carefully, keeps an eye on key objectives but also makes room for addressing the law firm's concerns and pays attention to how they behave affects both sides of the value equation, all the evidence suggests that opportunities for lasting improvements are well worth the effort.

A primer for sourcing LPO services

Danny Ertel

As expense pressures have grown and sourcing teams have developed more experience buying legal services, some GCs still worry about whether procurement really "gets" legal and understands their priorities. They hence opt to bring some operations and sourcing expertise into the legal department, so they can rely on their own resources. Consider what the choice looks like from the perspective of a senior in-house counsel, when faced with on offer of procurement's "help." To change their choice, procurement needs to understand why leading with a sourcing exercise is so unattractive to a GC, and explore other ways to help: Rather than simply reach for what is often the low-hanging fruit in other categories and seek to create competition among providers, try to find out what problems the GC really wants to solve. Chances are that "finding a cheaper law firm" is not high on their list of challenges.

If I agree to let procurement help	If I continue to resist
− They will want me to stop using my current set of trusted law firms − I will have to build new relationships, and it's just a really bad time − I will have to use someone unproven, who may not be as good (after all, they command a lower rate in the market) − I will have to teach them my business − If the new, cheaper firms make a mess, I'm still accountable − for really big, risky stuff	+ I preserve control and autonomy + I can apply my own professional judgment and expertise to assess providers + I continue to use lawyers I know, trust, and who have always come through for me (and whom I can call and say "I need this" and they'll deliver) + I can focus my time and attention to really important things + I can always agree to take another look at this when we're not really busy/under pressure to perform
+ I may save some money (but these bills don't even come out of my budget)	− I upset procurement

Legal departments need to understand where their spend is going and whether there is a better way to match resources to problems. They need to get smarter about leveraging technology, and to make use of more sophisticated pricing models than time and materials with a cap. Procurement can help with these and other tasks. An example of a less threatening, but nonetheless valuable way for procurement to assist the legal department is in an exploration of whether legal services can be "unbundled" and whether some activities traditionally carried out by counsel should be outsourced to legal process outsourcing companies (LPO). Legal departments actually have much more experience than many other functions outsourcing and working closely with outside providers (law firms). But unbundling activities that have traditionally been treated as single matters or services and determining how to move some tasks to other providers does create different risks to manage, ranging from scope definition and provider selection to the impact on the relationship with lead outside counsel.

Aligning around outsourcing objectives

Clarifying objectives is critical. What makes doing so more challenging in legal services is that non-financial objectives are often as important as cost savings. Identify those with rigor, so they do not become excuses for sloppy analysis, and develop ways to account for them in an outsourcing business case. The ways in which legal departments can obtain value by outsourcing has implications for the process:

- **Reduce internal headcount—by shifting activities to a third party:** This is the typical way in which other business functions save money by outsourcing. Given the size of a typical legal department, a headcount reduction objective means the scope of the LPO engagement will be relatively small. Initial engagements are often as small as 10 full-time equivalents (FTEs). Transition and governance costs must be contained, lest they overwhelm the business case. Clear role definitions and workflows are critical to enabling both customer and provider to understand the scope of work, price it, and determine whether there is sufficient value to incur accompanying risks. As a percentage of the company's total legal expenses, the potential savings from reducing the cost of a portion of its not-very-large legal department may not be very exciting. Alternative ways to achieve comparable savings, including automation, or just ceasing certain legal support activities may offer easier paths.

- **Reduce external spend—by shifting activities from outside counsel to an LPO:** This represents a much larger opportunity for savings and has different implications. Savings are realized on a matter-by-matter basis, often by a business unit budget holder; but there will be additional costs incurred by legal as overhead to manage a process that is more like "serial out-tasking" than traditional outsourcing. The most common example of this sort of outsourcing (which, incidentally, represents about 50% of the work of many LPO providers) involves sending initial document review work to a provider, but having outside counsel provide supervision and quality assurance. Savings are realized in comparison to having outside counsel conduct all of the review work, using a blend of their own associates and contract attorneys.

- **Shift internal resources to more value-adding priorities:** This produces savings by avoiding the cost of hiring additional staff, but it delivers a real benefit: making sure that in-house lawyers spend their time productively. Consider the value of freeing up legal staff from reviewing every routine change proposed by a counter-party to the thousands of non-disclosure agreements a technology company signs every year, where most of those proposed changes fall into one of a handful of predictable and acceptable requests that can be described in an outsourcer's playbook. Freeing up their time from mundane tasks is important to retaining motivated professionals and to making sure that the company realizes a return on its in-house legal talent. Translating this management objective into one that justifies the disruption and expense of a sourcing exercise, however, requires that legal department management articulate what priorities are underserved because of such unavoidable but lower value tasks.

- **Provide new, formerly unaffordable services to the business:** This falls on the side of "do more" rather than "with less." Companies face ever-increasing risks; outsourcing can allow legal to provide new or added risk management services to the business. The value here comes from reduced risks elsewhere in the company rather than savings in the legal department. The availability of lower cost resources, managed to a well-run process, and supported by effective technology can allow legal departments to provide support that might otherwise be unthinkable. E.g.: document detailed, market-by-market guidance about the legal and regulatory risks facing their distributors; extract key terms and conditions data from thousands of license agreements; review every piece of advertising copy for potential

Truth-in-Advertising violations; conduct due diligence reviews on every major customer contract for an acquisition target; and more.

Assessing the portfolio of opportunities

A joint procurement-legal team can map current legal spend and current in-house and outside counsel activities against a desired future state and determine what process and role changes may be required before (or as part of the transition phase of) an outsourcing engagement. The objectives should shape the way the review of activities is conducted. Keep in mind that:

- **Not all of the current activities need to be mapped forward.** Some activities may simply cease and others may be substituted for by automation. For example, Cisco's legal department's review of activities that could be eliminated or moved from their contract negotiators to a "low touch" or self-service model, zeroed in on basic information requests on contract content, providing comments on non-legal templates, a variety of documentation/ status updates, and more.

- **There are significant opportunities for value in some activities not done at all today.** Many processes in legal departments are created to manage risk within resource constraints. Under pressure to keep fixed costs down, they rely on law firms to recruit and manage talent year-round so that it is available when needed; but because their hourly rates seem high, clients often ask law firms to limit their efforts to what is necessary. When carrying out due diligence on an acquisition, for example, clients usually ask law firms to summarize as few documents as are necessary to provide and support their opinion. But after they close on the transaction, the acquirer usually finds that many more documents and more complete summaries would actually be quite useful for effective post-merger integration and management of acquired company, people, and assets. Those additional summaries would not show up on a current state map of the due diligence process, but represent an opportunity to gain additional value from integrating pre- and post-deal activities, something outsourcing can make affordable.

Considering the supplier market

The LPO market is still relatively immature. Few providers currently have sufficient business to develop the depth of experience they need or to afford the required investments. While there is nothing wrong with being a small provider, provider market intelligence will be a very important part of risk management. Keep in mind:

• The LPO supplier market structure implies that there is a list of the "usual suspects" who should at least be considered in most sourcing exercises: The top providers who have earned the confidence of the early adopters, have learned a lot along the way, and have made the necessary investments in security, business continuity, hiring, training, and more.

• Including some "dark horses" pays off: Depending on the processes in scope and the objectives of the legal department, there may be surprises in the analysis. For example, multi-line service providers could bring a different perspective, ask different questions, and credibly propose different solutions to the client's challenges. Or a comparatively small provider (for which due diligence confirms sufficient capital and critical mass to meet minimum requirements) with the desire and entrepreneurship to win a "lighthouse" account can do quite well.

Engaging with the supplier market

There has been enough news about LPOs and enough pressure on legal costs that some LPO sales teams receive lots of RFPs, many of which turn out to come from "tire kickers" who are not seriously considering outsourcing. Providers have had to learn to qualify opportunities more carefully and become choosier about whether and how they respond. Applying a few of these lessons learned will improve the likelihood that your RFP will get the kind of responses you need to make good choices:

- **Avoid sending generic requests.** As thinly spread bid-response teams look at incoming requests, they try to ascertain how serious the requester is. The more thought and care that seems to have gone into the RFP, the more likely they will interpret the opportunity as a real one.

- **Organize your request.** Facilitate providers' use of standard answers or exhibits to necessary but routine "due diligence" type questions (e.g., physical security policies; financial status and ownership structure; and any recent litigation) and allow them to focus their time and energy on their value-add solutions to your business needs. To ensure creative answers and realistic scoping, clearly describe your objectives, your current views on scope, and the way in which the work is accomplished today.

- **Don't ask them to "bid on your spreadsheet."** The market for LPO services is not sufficiently mature that all provider's contract management services, IP services, or document review services are alike. LPO services are at the more commoditized end of the legal services spectrum, but they are not actually commodities differentiated only by rates. The value proposition from a good LPO provider has to be about more than labor arbitrage. Their use of technology and effective process management and the quality of the people they hire and train will drive differences in quality, productivity, and error rates. Their experience solving similar problems will differentiate the creativeness of their solutions and their ability to implement them. Ensuring that your request allows providers to differentiate themselves on these things will help you realize the value of outsourcing these activities.

- **Give them a reasonable baseline.** You want providers to be able to "show off" what differentiates them, but you also need to be able to make direct comparisons. Hourly rates don't tell you about value for money and the number of hours they estimate for the work will vary more widely than their rates. For example, a legal department set up a data room with materials from a prior, already closed deal, and asked providers to use that data room as the basis for their estimates of what a comparable summarization exercise would cost. Providers were asked to "show their work" so that the evaluation team could understand how they went about developing their estimates and what assumptions went into it.

- **Insist on evidence of experience.** There is a learning curve in delivering legal support services and providers who cannot demonstrate that they have had sufficient experience, delivering sufficiently similar services, to sufficiently similar clients, should not get your business. Ask providers to describe what their experience has been in concrete terms: years delivering the service, volumes delivered, numbers of FTEs and teams, locations out of which they replicated their processes, etc. Ask for case studies and relevant references. Ask providers to describe how they ascertain the quality of their work and what their data shows.

Aligning around provider selection

Next, you will have to evaluate the responses, narrow down your selection, conduct additional due diligence, and negotiate terms with the leading candidate(s). While most of these activities are straightforward and familiar to sourcing professionals, keep in mind when sourcing LPO services:

- Legal and procurement bring different perspectives to the evaluation, and both are valuable. Adopt a framework to carry out the evaluation that allows teams to surface and discuss different perceptions of the relative merits of different provider responses.

- Assessment criteria should be tied back to the business objectives. Clarifying what "great" looks like for each criterion, and examples of low, medium, or high scores greatly facilitate the work of individual reviewers and their discussion afterwards. Defining assessment criteria and assigning them relative weights should be done carefully. Some characteristics are very important, such as the ability of a provider to protect the confidentiality of the documents to which they have access. That doesn't mean this criterion should have a high weighting in the scoring. A provider whose security is not good enough could never be selected, even if their price were the lowest or their solution were the most creative. On the other hand, those exceeding the requisite level of protection should not get more "credit" in the evaluation as that does not deliver more value and should not really offset a deficiency elsewhere in their bid. Criteria such as these should not be weighed alongside others like the pricing, fitness for purpose of their solution, or their maturity in providing similar solutions, but be treated as "pass/fail" criterion.

Portions of this article previously appeared in Outsourcing magazine, May-June 2011 issue. Used with permission of the author and Outsourcing magazine.

Strategic versus tactical buyers

Geraint Evans

Senior management today requires their legal teams to play a key role in the business and see commercial advice as important as legal advice. Procurement managers collaborate with the legal department to support the company's core business strategic aims and obtain the best mix of quality, relationship, and value. To ensure that both in-house counsel and the legal services suppliers feel engaged and enthusiastic about this commercial relationship, procurement has to perfect a tricky balancing act between existing relationships and an objective review of supply side options.

Traditional and tactical buyers

The maturity of the procurement professionals and the sophistication they apply to the buying process is reflected in the experience law firms have of the processes that are run by procurement. A traditional buyer might focus on the supplier terms & conditions (T&Cs) and the discounts available. They will not have a view of the overall business or even in-house legal objectives and might only act in a gatekeeper role, ensuring that the process runs smoothly. A tactical buyer is likely to have a greater influence on the process and will be focused on the price and cost savings—and for example, may employ an eAuction as a method to achieve these goals. They will also insist on the use of their (the buyer's) master service agreement (MSA) and T&Cs—which can be divisive or confrontational. Suppliers will be told that any contact outside of the process will render you liable to disqualification; that they are XX% more expensive than their nearest competitor and that the client's T&Cs contained in the invitation to tender (ITT) must be agreed to.

The antagonism which sometimes occurs through the tactical procurement approach is most apparent when it comes to the negotiation of MSAs or the standard terms and conditions that are applied to the relationship. In many MSAs, clients require their legal suppliers to accept some terms that are at best weighted in favor of the client, and at worst are a breach of the joint trust you would expect of a professional services adviser. Most corporates would say though that they are just protecting the interests of the business and ultimately their shareholders. Some of the most contentious include:

- **Conflicts:** Many client MSAs insist on the full details of the firms' policy and procedures for managing conflicts of interest. In addition, if there are changes to the policy, some clients require immediate notification of the change. In most instances, compliance with this request is straightforward for a legal supplier. This clause becomes more difficult if there are any restrictions to act: e.g. if a client insists that the firm must decline to undertake litigation brought or proposed to be brought against them, or take on projects involving other parties in their sector. In practice, no legal supplier is likely to bring an action against their most important clients. However, when clients ask legal suppliers to demonstrate their understanding of their business and sector, and then ask them not to act for a host of vertical and horizontal competitors or even suppliers, that is where problems arise.

- **IP-Standard Protection of IP Term:** Standard supplier terms retain the copyright and intellectual property rights (IPR) for documents and other work developed for clients. Some clients make the distinction between "Foreground" and "Background" IPR. Those that insist that any Intellectual Property Rights created as "Foreground IPR" vest in with the client. Other terms are even more restrictive such as insisting that all rights in any written documents produced for the client shall belong or vest with the client.

- **Limitation of liability:** Many legal suppliers look to limit their liability and include covering liability provisions for the following agents: individual partners, associates, counsels, other employees, service companies etc. Some clients request that there is no limitation in the liability of the legal supplier and in some instances the MSAs will explicitly reference that there will be no limit to a supplier's liability.

- **Payment terms:** Supplier standard payment terms can range widely, but are typically around 30 days following the issuing of the final invoice. In the legal sector, clients' payment terms range from 45 days to 60 days, and even 120 days.

Strategic buyers

The strategic buyer will focus on the overall strategy and key objectives of the business and the legal teams, and will ensure that the process is driven by the business needs. Strategic buyers will have insight into the category supply market, and understand how this is changing through Alternative Business Structures (ABS), near-sourcing, Legal Process Outsourcing (LPO), AFAs and new entrants. Their approach will be to ensure that the procurement process combines "fit for purpose" suppliers with the strategic relationship management of the internal in-house client. When a client takes a strategic approach to the procurement of their legal services, this does not immediately mean that the process needs to be complex and highly involved. Some global panel reviews have taken a simplified form that has enabled in-house and procurement teams to focus on the critical objectives the business has, and avoid the lengthy and costly processes that have been seen since the legal services category came under the spotlight of professional purchasing. Clients ask legal suppliers to complete simplified questionnaires that cover the core information such as: international coverage; work-type coverage; agreed MSA principles and simplified blended rate cards. These questionnaires have formed the main element of a process that has saved time (and money) on behalf of the client and legal services suppliers.

Strategic buyers will be directly involved in the entire buying process: preparation, engagement, and delivery. Preparation may include category positioning, supply market analysis, customer segmentation, risk/cost analysis, contract model options, and scenario planning.

Let's look at **category positioning** as a way of comparing suppliers and preventing the criticism of some firms that clients are comparing "apples with pears." Frequently, law firms state "we don't compete with firm X" or "we're in a different league to firm Y" and discount those firms as competitors. However, this disregards the idea that clients themselves are using an increasingly diverse portfolio of legal services providers and that they may not categorize their legal suppliers in the same way law firms do. Category positioning is a way in which buyers differentiate their suppliers to reflect their needs as a business, rather than using firm directory rankings, number of lawyers or offices etc.

Strategic purchasers using category positioning assess the market using four quadrants: They will divide the market in high/low business impact and market difficulty as well as high/low percentage of expenditure. This will determine how they will engage with suppliers, and the overall purchasing strategy: are they aiming to secure strategically critical purchases? Or are they looking for efficiency? The underlying intent is to develop a differentiated strategy for each category of spend depending on a number of factors, such as supply market complexity, internal complexity, risks, savings opportunity, and various other factors that are unique to each organization.

The test for procurement is to understand where the supplier sits based on the volume of expenditure and the impact on the business—if the supplier was removed or was not able to provide the service and an alternative needed to be sourced. Suppliers that operate in a high "business impact and market difficulty" area where the company has a high percentage of expenditure are managed and developed in a very different way to those that operate in a low "business impact and market difficulty" area where the company has a low percentage of spend. This assessment is an almost exclusively internal. The assessment of suppliers relies upon the management information (MI) collated on the legal suppliers and the views on how critical and substitutable the service provided is.

Strategic purchasers also understand that suppliers undertake a similar approach to their clients, engaging with them in different ways. Strategic purchasers will assess how each supplier views them as a client and will adjust their purchasing approach accordingly. Are they highly attractive as a client—or not? Do they account for a high or low percentage of sales? In other words, are they "core" clients (high attractiveness, high sales), "development" clients (high attractiveness, low sales)? Or are they "exploitable" (low attractiveness, high sales), or even a "nuisance" (low attractiveness, low sales)?

Law firms and their clients might not necessarily categorize their clients and legal supplier relationships in such as formalized way. However, these frameworks can help explain why law firms and clients often misalign their objectives, and feel that panel reviews and project tenders result in sometimes difficult and confrontational discussions, rather than a mutually beneficial commercial relationship based on trust and openness.

Most large law firms have key account management (KAM) programs in place. The purpose is to manage the relationships with the firm's key clients in a more coordinated and commercial manner to generate profitable revenues from clients that the law firm wishes to keep and develop. As part of these KAM programs, clients will be assessed on an annual basis against a series of metrics that will often include the volume and/or percentage of sales from that client, and the attractiveness of that client (based on a mix of work type, brand recognition, people development and also revenue less cost of sales such as write offs, secondments, training, time invested in provision of MI and other added value benefits). As a result, law firms prioritize their resources against those clients that provide either greatest "development" opportunities or are "core" to the business.

When clients use category positioning frameworks and firms use similar client segmentation frameworks, it is possible that their views do not align. The worst case scenario for the client would be a strategically critical or strategic security supplier that sees the client in their nuisance or exploitable categories. On the flip side, a firm that sees the client in the development or core category while the client sees the legal supplier in the tactical acquisition or tactical profit category, is likely to experience some of the typical tactical approaches outlined earlier, or may even be removed from the panel, replaced by alternative providers that they may not have been aware of.

How long does it take to make changes to this document?

D. Casey Flaherty

Most legal work is performed on a computer. As corporate counsel and a buyer of legal services, I always worry: How much time is wasted (and billed) because lawyers are deficient in using basic software tools? To test my hypothesis about the lack of technological proficiency, I developed mock assignments for associates. These assignments have them refine a redlined agreement in Word, sift through a corporate database export in Excel, and prepare an e-filing in PDF. The specific tasks are of little importance—they are designed to test general basic skills. What is important is that the law firms have fared poorly.

The premise of the audit is that high-value resources should not waste time on low-value work. Still, I never tested a senior partner's tech utilization because they should not be doing the kind of work to begin with. Delegation remains crucial. Any suggestion that most drudgery is delegated to non-billable staff does not comport with the reality that non-billable staff is being reduced in record numbers. With every reduction in force, the attorney-to-staff ratios keep jumping—from 3:1 to 5:1 to 8:1—and the arithmetic of delegation becomes less plausible. How can a single secretary handle all of the labor-intensive work for multiple attorneys? The only viable explanation is that the secretary is substantially more skilled at using technology. This, however, assumes a much higher degree of staff tech proficiency than the evidence supports. It is also an admission that (a) the machine is doing the work and (b) the attorney does not know how to use the machine. My results suggest the attorneys do not know how to use the machine and are doing this work themselves anyway.

During my own years in BigLaw, I was shocked at how much time high-value resources dedicated to, and billed for, low-value work. In the quest for quality, partners, associates, and paralegals spent hours struggling to get documents just right. The objectives were righteous, the approach was flawed. Contracts and settlement agreements, for example, were far more labor intensive than necessary. The slightest edit—delete a clause here, add a provision there—necessitated a thorough revisiting of the document to ensure the numbering and cross-references were accurate. Of course, there is already an app for that—Word has automatic numbering and cross-references. Yet, someone not familiar with these automatic features can easily spend over two hours updating a contract after a new provision is added. This brute-force approach can also introduce hundreds of opportunities for errors—a missed cross-reference or typo—the machine would never make.

In transitioning to in-house, I regularly face the conundrum of choosing among multiple qualified firms when selecting outside counsel. Efficacy is a given, efficiency is a mystery. Given my own experience, I doubt claims of efficiency. Lacking data to make an informed decision, I devised a way to generate it myself: I created and conducted an in-person audit of firms' knowledge management, workflow, technology, and technology utilization. My objective was to ascertain, to the extent I could, how exactly my work would be handled. I conducted my audit at nine firms, most of them in the AmLaw 100.

Thus, I was unsurprised by the poor results in technology utilization. I had created a number of mock assignments based on my own time in BigLaw. The assignments were designed to test whether the individuals performing the lower-level work—associates, paralegals, secretaries—utilized the labor-saving features built into ubiquitous software like Outlook, Word, and Excel. What took me 30 minutes, took them 5 hours (median and mean) at an average billable rate of $270/hr. Such little inefficiencies aggregate into a staggering amount of time unintentionally wasted. Detours into drudgery sap precious focus from areas where legal professionals add real value. The driving force is ignorance paired with diligence in an environment where time is recoupable from the client. In most cases, the ignorance is so complete that practitioners simply don't know what they don't know and therefore operate under delusions of adequacy.

Articles about my audit results struck a nerve. From the resulting buzz, I gained a partner in Professor Andrew Perlman, head of Suffolk Law's Institute on Law Practice Technology & Innovation. Andy and I worked with a board of advisors to automate and enhance the technology-utilization piece of the original audit. The Suffolk/Flaherty Legal Tech Audit (LTA) was born. The LTA is administered on the user's own computer. The software walks the user through a continuous workflow that assesses proficiency with Word, Excel, and PDFs. The users receive their scores at the task level to identify deficiencies, train up, and retake the LTA. Most importantly, clients can request the outside counsel scores of their existing outside counsel or make score submittal part of their procurement process.

None of the individual tasks on the LTA require more than a minute. Cumulatively, the target time is 35 minutes, with expert users needing less than 15 minutes. Done incorrectly—without using labor-saving features—tasks can take over an hour, and the complete LTA could, theoretically, eat up 10 hours. The LTA is not a game of gotcha. The objective is for legal professionals to take the LTA, identify deficiencies, and get appropriate training. That training is widely available; the problem is that legal professionals don't take advantage of it.

The challenge is to convince someone to give up billable time to take non-billable training in order to reduce future hours billed. The sole sure method to change behavior is to actually change behavior. I believe that it will require client pressure to shift the profession from low-proficiency equilibrium to a high-proficiency equilibrium. To apply that pressure, clients will need to demand objective, empirical data like the LTA and incorporate such metrics into a rational purchase process. Improper utilization of basic technology is not the biggest problem facing the legal industry. But it is a very real problem with significant financial and quality consequences. It is also among the easiest problems to solve. Objective measures like the LTA give clients a mechanism to hold firms accountable and improve the way we all buy legal.

Saving the "Trusted Advisor" relationship

Charles H. Green

Many lawyers decry the presence of legal procurement, saying it amounts to commoditization of the profession, and ruins the chances for the development of deep trust-based relationships between counsel and their clients. The legal profession has probably reacted no worse than the consulting profession before them, and engineers before them, to be subjected to the procedures of procurement. The smarter and cooler heads, however, recognize it as the emerging way things are, and determine to work with the new situation.

From the client's side, things can look different. Some companies who have embraced procurement have found it can generate massive reductions in fees, while actually increasing quality and responsiveness. From their perspective, the term "trusted advisor" is too often a sham, covering up all-too-cozy relationships, shielding law firms from the disinfecting sunlight of competition, and delivering over-priced legal services of dubious quality. A trusted advisor is characterized by a wide range of capabilities including Credibility, Reliability, Intimacy, and a low level of Self-Orientation, and by actions consistently guided by client focus first, collaboration, a relationship rather than transactional perspective, and an inclination toward transparency. A trusted advisor relationship also requires a propensity to trust on the part of the client. A constantly suspicious client will never engage a trusted advisor in the first place, nor allow a trusted advisor relationship to develop.

Benefits of "Trusted Advisor" relationships: The relationship between trusting and trusted revolves around risk. The client must be willing to take certain risks, and the advisor must be willing to reciprocate, in great part by suppressing his own needs for immediate self-gratification. An advisor who focuses solely on risk mitigation will lose his advisees. A trusted advisor who never himself takes any risks will quickly cease to be trusted. The benefits of trusted advisor relationships accrue to both the advisor and the advisee. When a client can trust an advisor, advice can be taken without lengthy questioning or doubting. Contracts are quickly secured by handshake. The client is assured of the client-focused intentions of the advisor at all times. If asked to give advice on a subject outside the advisor's area of expertise, a trusted advisor will seek out sources that offer what he cannot, rather than abuse the privilege.

Trusted advisor relationships are more profitable for the advisor mainly because the cost of sales is reduced. This is partly due to repeat business, and partly due to absence of a felt desire on the part of the client to investigate other sources. But they are also more profitable to the client. Being able to depend on a competent trusted advisor means you can sole source when you want to, and be assured that you'll go out to bid when you have to. It means you will not be taken advantage of by unscrupulous or predatory pricing. Most importantly, it means that the advisor's interests are always your own. This lowers risk, time to market, the cost of contracting, and the cost of insuring against bad performance. It means you will be told the hard truths when you need to hear them, but be told them in a way that is not hostile, but instead supportive. One of the biggest advantages of a trusted advisor relationship is the knowledge that comes with time. It stands to reason that work split among three advisors will potentially be more expensive per unit; more importantly, each advisor will have less of a picture of the whole than if one advisor is consistently exposed to the thoughts and workings of the client organization.

Risks of "Trusted Advisor" relationships: Someone operating as a trusted advisor is a fiduciary, a professional, someone dedicated to the highest levels of client service. There are very few risks to anyone when lawyers behave in that manner, other than to the lawyer himself if he naively misreads some highly unscrupulous clients. It can be tempting for the advisor to take the relationship for granted, to not hustle quite so much, to pad the bill a little bit, or even to shade the advice to suit the client's wishes, rather than tell a difficult truth. The slide down this slippery slope can start with the advisor, or equally with the client, wishing to make things easier for someone who feels like a friend. When this happens, the advisor reaps excessive fees; the advice becomes tainted; the client is denied the freshness of competing perspectives; and the advisor's motives become suspect. A true trusted advisor will guard against this happening.

"Trusted Advisor" vs. procurement
Given the above, it's easy to see where the approach to procurement can prevent a trusted advisor relationship. Procurement processes are (rightly) skeptical. Procurement's job includes asking tough questions of vendors. This puts them in the position of appearing to be more risk-averse than their internal clients. The biggest hurdle is that procurement tends to see a series of transactions, and to be suspicious of relationships. But if three law firms are constantly competing against each other for every job, there is little room for the development of a

holistic perspective, little incentive for the advisor to develop staff particularly for the client, and little the client can do to reward continued selfless service. The procurement process itself has yet to integrate this fundamental perspective.

The role of the legal department: It's easy to forget that purchasing outside legal services is always done in the context of a strategic decision—whether or not to retain those services in-house. The procurement function must respect that strategic decision by the legal department, and not push hard enough to destroy the viability of going outside if the legal department is not ready to take the work in-house. Clients, like advisors, are prone to extremes. Some may be too risk-averse, or become obsessed with the need to appear "fair," or put undue stress on the need to "keep them off balance" by viewing the vendor relationship solely in power terms. Getting too cozy with an advisory firm is only one pathology; the inability to form solid relationships with outside firms can ultimately be more risky than the propensity to form those relationships. The client who handles vendor relationships right will have a point of view that consciously balances the power relationships, the health of the vendors involved, the scale economies available, and the risks of overly focusing. (Government clients are of course different, being generally obliged to entertain multiple vendors). In that context, a trusted advisor relationship can and often does make a great deal of strategic sense.

The role of procurement: Outside law firms are often given to conspiratorial views about the role of procurement within the client organization. They would be surprised to find that many in the procurement function feel similarly put upon by internal clients who insist on hammering out deals themselves, leaving "purchasing" to "nail down a good price with them," or to "squeeze them until they squeal." Historically, procurement has pushed for a view of itself as cutting costs. There are several reasons for this: costs are easy to measure, they are susceptible to being defined in creative ways, they are relatively easy to manage, and "cost-cutting," while no organization's idea of a good time, is something well understood and tolerated up to some point.

The problem is, and good procurement people know this, that cost-cutting is not the most strategic way to view procurement. Return on investment analysis, by which procurement is held accountable for total "spend," is a far more appropriate way to view its capabilities. To think about total spend is to measure returns on something, rather than simply deductions from something; and to measure over larger periods of time than merely budgetary periods. The other strategic issue is that procurement has yet to grapple with placing a value on relationships. It is easier to manage a process which is repeated transaction by transaction. But just as sales models that operate in a relationship vacuum are bound to underperform relationship-based models, so too is procurement underperforming if it continues to duck the issue of valuing relationships.

Getting "Trusted Advisor" relationships wrong
Each party—the law firm, the legal department, and procurement—need to guard against certain inclinations:

- **The firm** must guard against complacency, taking things for granted. It must continue to develop new staff to serve the client, continue to aggressively balance strong personal relationships with the integrity to call out the truth when it's painful. It must be willing to turn down business if another source would better serve the client. And, it must be willing to leave the client if it becomes unethical to meet their demands.

- **The legal department** must be willing to take risks and to be completely transparent. A trusted advisor relationship can only benefit the client if the advisor is kept in the loop. Like the advisor, the client must be willing to take a long-term view of things and forego the luxury of selectively changing policies. For example, if outside legal expenditures are the first to go in an economic downturn, and this has not been previously discussed, the relationship will be strained.

- **The procurement function:** In addition to its job of working with vendors, procurement must effectively market itself within the firm as a trusted advisor, rather than be an order-taker for cost-cutting pressure. Having done so successfully, the biggest challenges are moving from costs metrics to spend metrics, and to allow for real value provided from valid trusted advisor relationships.

Procurement needs a new metric

Charles H. Green

Bill Young

Six areas of conflict demonstrate how procurement's targets and metrics serve to defeat its strategic aims and undermine the work. These include incentives to engage late with vendors, to over-specify requirements, and to shrink a business rather than grow it. There is a need for an alternative to savings as the main reporting metric for procurement—the spend control index (SCI).

Procurement is intended to support the strategic aims of the organization. However, colleagues in other departments are confused about procurement's role and intentions and hence don't trust procurement's motives. This is due to misunderstandings and a good bit is procurement's own fault. Whilst presenting itself as a strategic business partner, some purchasing practices are tactical—and worse yet, self-serving. This creates a trust issue both internally and externally. The reasons for lack of trust show up in procurement's target metrics and the way in which procurement reports them. The metrics are excessively focused on savings, even when those savings are secondary or cannot be measured. While savings are a proper target for certain cost-down programs, the aggregated total of savings is a misleading performance indicator. Its acceptance and use create perverse incentives.

The tensions are an outcome of two distinct views of sourcing outside services: one is rooted in transactions, the other based on relationships. A solution lies in better defining procurement's transactional vs. relationship responsibilities, using a performance indicator superior to cost savings. Procurement has also shifted from a tactical function to a strategic one. This has brought the potential of confusion between its traditional tactical role and its new strategic role, which can lead to six areas of conflict:

1. **Price vs. value assessments:** Procurement often helps budget owners to understand a need better, identify the best goods and services for that need, and undertake cost/benefit analyses for different solutions. When there are more factors to consider than price alone, procurement uses weighted criteria to evaluate the best offer. While this help may be appreciated, procurement's target and own performance criteria are based mainly on achieved savings. This means they have an incentive to push hardest on price rather than other factors that contribute to value. The effect is that intentions are unclear, incentives are mixed, and budget owners are confused, even resentful.

2. **Market-based solutions:** Procurement typically challenges price through competitive tendering. This is based on a faith in the rational outcomes of markets. The aim of procurement then is to formalize the requirements, remove subjectivity, and bring the service as close to a commodity as possible. In practice, we use

rational criteria in the screening part of a down-selection process to create a shortlist of suppliers, all of whom are qualified to provide the required goods or services. But then we look the supplier candidates in the eye to decide which one we would like to deal with. This final selection stage is less cognitively-defined and less tangible. Senior managers are paid to make judgments, while procurement's aim is to remove intangibles like trust from the vendor-selection process. This works well in the first phase of screening, but when it comes to the selection phase, client managers want to explore a relationship with the final candidates and test their own comfort level before moving forward.

3. **Explicit vs. implicit contracts:** Explicit contracts are written and formal, while implicit contracts are usually created during a working relationship and are based on trust. Often the two go together: the explicit contract is agreed between the organizations at the start; and implicit deals, based on trust, develop between individuals working together. Procurement worries about cozy relationships that circumvent the formal buying process and tries to over-formalize; it may fail to recognize that implicit deals are essential. It may even go further, towards the deliberate exploitation of a vendor's trust and the breaking of implicit deals.

4. **Strategic differences:** Chief Procurement Officers (CPO) say their staff should become involved in projects earlier and more strategically, so they can drive efficiencies and cost avoidance during the planning and design stages of projects, not just during final vendor negotiations. They recruit and develop purchasing managers with higher-level skills, who can work strategically with their clients' functional leadership teams. But these strategic discussions raise a tension when it comes to measuring performance. Procurement performance is typically measured by cost savings and few CPOs offer an alternative. Unfortunately,

pursuing strategic objectives can lower the possible range of savings targets.

Here's how: At first, everyone agrees on the value of early, strategic engagement. It creates clarity of the business issue, sharper specifications, more appropriate technical solutions, and earlier screening out of unsuitable suppliers. But this narrows the delta which procurement is able to report as a saving. With a smaller number of qualified suppliers, the gap between the highest and lowest bidder is reduced and it is even possible that the highest bidder offers the best overall value. How, if they are rewarded mainly on savings, is the procurement manager incentivized to invest time and effort in strategy?

5. **Contrived calculations:** Continued use of transaction-based metrics to evaluate strategic objectives can lead to serious gaming of the system. For example, procurement savings on raw materials can be translated into P&L accounts only if there are on-going purchases and like-for-like unit-price comparisons. In legal, this is typically not the case, so procurement looks for reportable savings in:

   - The difference between two quotes
   - External benchmarks
   - Internal changes (e.g. job cuts)
   - Other benefits (e.g. production efficiencies, waste reduction, reduced working capital)

These calculations have a subjective element but are nevertheless aggregated with unit-price reductions to create the headline number reported by the CPO. Reported savings also address only the areas that procurement chooses to report. A price rise is likely to go unreported so there is a perverse incentive for procurement to farm expenditure, like a crop in a field: allowing the crop to grow longer (and let prices rise) to get a better harvest (of savings). Executives know that reported aggregate savings are not real, but they accept that cost reductions are generally desirable and pretend that the reported savings are meaningful.

6. **Operating budgets vs. strategic spending:** Some organizations translate savings into budget cuts, especially those where procurement reports through finance. Not surprisingly, managers may be disinclined to accept support from procurement if their operating budget is reduced as a consequence. Budget-owners who did not previously voice their doubts about procurement's reported savings may speak up when their own budget is threatened in order to deliver buyers' bonuses.

All six of these areas of conflict have in common that they arise because there is one metric on which procurement expects to be measured. It emphasizes aggregate total cost reductions, savings, above everything else when presenting its performance and promoting its value to the organization.

Procurement needs a new KPI, one that aligns procurement with the interests of its internal clients and allows it to build the trust: let's call it a spend control index (SCI). Instead of focusing attention only on active negotiations—and restricting reporting to live projects—the aim is to make procurement accountable for all spend. This uses a top-down measure of external spend, derived from turnover, adjusted for salaries, earnings, interest, extraordinary activities, depreciation, and working capital. Using this base (100% of spend), the proportion of spend that is actively and fully managed by procurement according to a strategy agreed with the business is reported. Key questions of control for each item of spend include:

- Is there an identified procurement manager with accountability for ensuring that the item is efficiently and effectively sourced and that purchase transactions follow the correct channels? Is this person recognized by the business as the point of escalation for purchasing issues?

- Is the item covered by a procurement strategy that is documented, less than twelve months old, and formally agreed with the budget owner?

- Is there an internal communications document to inform users how to acquire the goods or services? Are users instructed on how to find this document, how to deal with the vendor, and how to escalate issues?

- Is there an identified manager who is accountable for ensuring that the item is delivered and used according to the agreement and in line with business requirements? This person may be called a contract manager, vendor manager, or service manager, and they are usually line-managed by the budget owner, rather than being in the procurement department.

- Are the correct procurement channels and transactions being used? Reporting the proportion of total spend that is under control gets real attention from the executive team and relegates tactical savings to second place.

Maximizing the SCI aligns procurement with business objectives and internal audit can check it. It is not even necessary for procurement to manage everything hands-on. In the same way that the legal function is accountable for an organization's legal compliance but does not have to be present in every business meeting, procurement's role no longer needs to be so interfering.

Research report: Legal & procurement in Germany

Markus Hartung

Arne Gärtner

Legal procurement has become a vital function to manage spend among leading companies in Germany. As spend management is part of legal operation's responsibility, we found that procurement has evolved to being a support function to legal operations. Clear allocation of tasks and responsibilities is important. An integral part of this support is a know-how transfer on procurement issues.

Legal departments have significantly increased their management skills. This is one of the key insights we have gleaned from our two research studies on legal departments in 2012 and 2014. Companies expect their GCs to think and act like business people. And so the GCs improved the efficiency and effectiveness of their departments. We also noticed a move away from individual measures to cut costs to a more strategic and systematic approach, and we noticed more sharing of responsibilities and delegation.

GCs used to be solely responsible for legal management and operations but realized that they cannot be in charge of every aspect of legal management and operations and fulfill their duties as chief legal advisers at the same time. An increasing number of Chief Operation Officers (COO) Legal hence support GCs in major German companies to manage spend, supply chains, knowledge, staff, processes, and projects. They help to get rid of organizational slacks as well. In Germany, procurement of legal services is a key function of legal operations.

When we first looked into this topic two years ago, we interviewed German GCs about their long-term goals, their key strategic objectives, and the role of procurement departments. We came to the conclusion that participation of procurement departments (in the procurement of legal services) is not an isolated occurrence. We identified three main goals of GCs: cost cutting, reduction of complexity and increased efficiency. While cost cutting is a short-term measure to save money, reduction of complexity means that GCs had to get rid of organizational slack within legal departments. To increase efficiency, processes had to be established. GCs relied on a set of different instruments to achieve these goals:

- Reduce the number of law firms they work closely with
- Instruct smaller law firms and boutiques more frequently
- Negotiate fee arrangements
- Establish panels
- Develop their own international network
- Establish a global matrix-organization

Some of these instruments were new in 2012. Today they are common in legal departments and became a part of legal operations. In 2012 it was also still unclear which role procurement would play in the long run. Procurement was involved in the buying of legal services to negotiate fees with law firms (procurement acting as "bad cop") and to act as partners of legal departments, helping with the development of procurement criteria, the selection of law firms, the need analysis, and requests for proposals. Procurement also participated in pitches and helped evaluate the performance of law firms in terms of a cost-benefit analysis. Procurement should help legal operations with the design and optimization of legal procurement processes. Nevertheless, procurement has little influence on the selection of law firms. And was procurement here to stay? GCs who focused on cost savings usually involved the procurement department to negotiate the fees. But GCs who pursued a long-term strategy and wanted to reduce complexity and increase efficiency saw the role of the procurement department as partner of the legal department. They valued procurement's know-how on sourcing processes in their quest to become more efficient.

At the same time, some GCs did not see the connection between legal and procurement departments as a long-lasting relationship and treated it as a simple know-how transfer: They were eager to learn and understand everything procurement could teach them and then internalize this knowledge. Our assumption is therefore that legal departments might aspire to become "independent" again, believing that they no longer need procurement.

Division of labor in modern legal departments: Key success factors of legal management are the division of labor within the legal department and a clear approach to allocation of tasks and responsibilities. As part of our research, we examined the division of labor in modern legal departments and came to the conclusion that GCs today are much more than excellent lawyers, they also have to be great managers and leaders. In addition to traditional tasks such as the (re)active provision of legal services, proactive risk management, and being the trusted advisor to the board, they need to find the most efficient and effective way to allocate tasks and responsibilities within the department. A strategic approach to multi-sourcing is mandatory, including alternative providers of legal services. GCs support collaboration between practice groups and prevent internal competition. They also ensure collaboration between the legal department and other departments within the company.

GCs in modern legal departments understand that they cannot master all aspects of management on their own. They establish lean management structures and processes within the legal department that help to manage the department in the most efficient way. To focus on their core duties, GCs share some of the responsibilities with the COO Legal. This division of labor leads to a further increase in professionalism and efficiency within legal departments. Modern legal departments manage legal operations that comprises of five core activities:

- Project management
- Knowledge management
- Spend management
- Supply chain management, and
- Continuing process optimization.

GCs also need to set up a good governance structure to manage all these responsibilities. These activities are hence often under "legal operations" with a head of legal operations/COO Legal in charge. This function typically reports directly to the GC. COO Legal focus on managing legal operations and—together with the GC—set the department's strategy regarding size and shape, make-or-buy strategy, multi-sourcing approach, and legal IT. They must have a profound understanding of legal markets and the legal services industry, in particular of supply side of the market. The COO Legal is also responsible for innovation and change management. This division of labor is only possible when GCs learn to delegate tasks and responsibilities, which more and more do. In fact, our research shows that most legal departments are on their way to a clear division of labor between the GC and the COO Legal. This is only possible when the relationship between the GC and the COO Legal is characterized by trust and mutual respect.

How to win GSK's business

Dr. Silvia Hodges Silverstein

"'Who the heck are these guys?' That's probably the most common thing procurement people used to hear when they tried to break into the legal space," laughs Justin Ergler, director of alternative fee intelligence and analytics at GlaxoSmithKline (GSK). "Now, many companies involve procurement in buying legal services. Having us at the negotiation table is no longer the exception. No firm in their right mind can say today 'we don't deal with procurement.' It's no longer an option."

In just a few years, legal procurement has come a long way. Top management mandates procurement to help the legal department with strategies, processes, and tools to rein in spending while maintaining excellent legal representation. As an industry rule of thumb, involving procurement typically reduces outside counsel spend by 15-20%. It is no surprise that the majority of Fortune 500 companies now have professionals tasked with sourcing legal services and helping to manage relationships with firms, particularly big legal spenders like financial services and banking, the pharmaceutical industry, and technology companies. GSK is among legal procurement's most prominent pioneers. In 2013, my co-researcher Heidi K. Gardner and I authored a Harvard Business School case (see end of article) on the pharmaceutical company's advances in legal procurement.

Still, not everybody is a fan. Legal procurement often faces strong resistance from outside counsel who would like to circumvent procurement. Some firms bemoan procurement's involvement in buying legal services, wishing that legal alone should hire law firms. "Firms need to understand that GSK is your client; not just the in-house attorneys at GSK," says Ergler. And then there are in-house counsel who prefer making their own law firm choices, without support from their colleagues in procurement. "Legal services used to be the final frontier for procurement officers because the conventional wisdom was that you needed to be a lawyer to understand what the law department is sourcing," says Ergler. Marty Harlow, Ergler's predecessor in legal procurement readily tells the story that he was kicked out of numerous meetings with the legal department: "You need thick skin for this job."

Under Harlow, procurement had its first successes in buying legal services. Procurement had to first understand what corporate legal departments do and what law firms do. They had to learn the ins and outs from eDiscovery, court reporting, and trial phases to relevant landmark patent cases. Harlow led an initiative to analyze numerous outside counsel selection decisions with the goal of better understanding how GSK paid for outside counsel and why particular law firms were used. Unless procurement knows which questions to ask and is able to look at a proposal from a law firm and flag issues, the door to the legal department remains closed, Ergler believes.

Before buying legal services, Ergler had sourced a variety of products and services, from raw materials for consumer health care products, packaging, to IT, and marketing services. But nothing had prepared him for understanding how different buying legal services would be. "The relationships between company folks and vendors in other categories are nowhere near as strong as the relationships between in-house attorneys and outside counsel," says Ergler. In-house attorneys and outside counsel often went to the same law schools, worked for the same law firms; they have known each other for many years. This fosters very strong relationships. "We are talking about real relationships here, not just professional relationships," says Ergler. Because of this, outside counsel have significantly more power than suppliers in any other category. This makes procurement's job of partnering with the legal department to make buying decisions much more difficult. It is, however, possible to breakthrough with "value added" insight.

At GSK, legal procurement started with sourcing ancillary litigation services, including court reporting, medical records, document collection and review, and copying services. It saved GSK $23 million after Harlow's initial negotiations and improved service which GSK continuously measured, resulting in standardized quality benchmarks. The initial successes sparked further development into "real" legal services with GSK's new GC Dan Troy. Troy had the CEO's mandate to significantly reduce outside legal spend while getting excellent legal representation. A firm believer that the hourly-rate billing system can promote inefficiency, Troy appointed long-time GSK in-house lawyer Bob Harchut to head the new Global External Legal Relations Team (GELRT). Harchut built a cross-functional team that included procurement, finance, IT, and a Lean Six Sigma project manager to develop tools and processes. GELRT's mission was to change the way GSK paid for legal services: Outside counsel assignments had to be non-hourly, value-based (alternative) fee arrangements. Troy expected firms to put some 'skin in the game' to help GSK meet their cost savings goals, but insisted on a 'win-win:' both the client and the firm had to strike a balance that provided GSK with excellent legal representation/ favorable outcomes while the firm worked as efficiently as possible and maintained its profitability.

Senior management strongly supported the GELRT/legal procurement relationship: Troy reasoned that he had to "spend a little to save a lot," regularly tracked the progress and communicated successes within the legal department and to the company at large. GSK's in-house lawyers liked that procurement could relieve them of some unpleasant work: negotiations with law firms, in particular about price. Ergler believes that "lawyers want to be lawyers, and doing lawyers' work. They generally don't like talking about fees, negotiating price with outside counsel." The collaboration with procurement also allows the legal department to show the CEO and CFO that they are being good stewards of the company's money. It didn't hurt, says Ergler, that annual evaluations of GSK's in-house lawyers were linked to their contributions to GELRT's progress.

The next step for legal procurement was to get involved in the selection process of law firms for actual legal matters as opposed to simply selecting "preferred panels." At GSK, legal procurement and GELRT worked closely together and collaborated with the in-house attorneys to create a sourcing process for larger, more complex legal matters— defined as those over $250,000—like product liability litigation, corporate transactions, and patent litigation matters. The team mapped out the tools and processes in detail with corresponding resources. "We learned early on that it is essential to identify the assumptions that go into the matter and agree to those with our firms. Those assumptions form the basis for going forward," says Ergler. "By having an upfront understanding of how we think the matter will play out, GSK can reduce the complexity and uncertainty in legal matters. Still, if a material change occurs, we will be flexible."

Ergler is critical of procurement functions that treat legal like any other category: He advises new legal procurement professionals to translate and adjust their procurement tools to the legal world. "'Reverse auctions' sounded too harsh for the legal world, so that became 'sourcing rooms,'" explains Ergler. Procurement should also not be—or try to be—in a position where they actually select law firms. "We add structure and process to buying legal services. We provide rigor, we provide decision-grade data. We show value." RFPs that were used in other areas should be tailored to the legal department's needs. Ergler thinks nothing of 300-plus question RFPs. "Who is going to read all this? That is just making firms jump through hoop after hoop. If I was in a law firm, unless you are on preferred panel, have another 'in' or someone is really trying to develop the relationship, I'd throw such an RFP into the trash."

Ergler also advises law firms to find out exactly what the client is asking for. "Don't give a 'canned' marketing answer," he says. "If we ask you about specific matters, show us how you are "closest to the pin." Tell us about your specific experience for this particular matter. Have you litigated a similar issue for a peer client in this particular jurisdiction? That's what we want to know. Give us the best team that can solve our issues. Do not tell us about your Chambers rankings in the general area." Clients like GSK want to see that the firm has put in some thought and is able to explain why it is more beneficial for GSK to work with them on this specific matter rather than telling in many ways how wonderful the firm is in general.

To get on the winning side with GSK, Ergler advises law firms to have business people on staff that show the client that the firm is really aligned with them on a business level. More and more firms have done just that, hired business people, pricing directors with similar analytical backgrounds who speak procurement's language and are used to focusing on business metrics like Ergler and his peers. "Invest in your business side," urges Ergler. "Understand fees, understand cost. Otherwise, firms will usually send partners who have to do something they don't want to do and haven't had to do it often." It makes it difficult for Ergler to trust the numbers of firms where non-financially trained lawyers present the numbers. "I need to understand how you came up with your fee proposal. Be able to explain your logic to me, show me your data." Senior business people on the law firm side with decision-grade data instill trust that the firm put in the right effort to make an informed fee proposal.

"Some firms are very aligned with us, light years ahead of others," says Ergler. Those are best positioned to gain more and more business in the future. Ergler believes that in other firms, archaic compensation models stifle innovation. "If we don't pay hours times rate, but a flat fee instead—the more efficient the firm, the more profit it can make. Many law firm compensation models can be in direct conflict with how they reward their attorneys." Firms that have resisted change at every turn are beginning to see opportunities decrease as those hungry and willing to compete do their homework. "Some relationships with long-standing law firms have changed. But law firms have the opportunity, the ball is in their court. Continue to stick your head in the sand or face the new reality," says Ergler.

About the Harvard Business School case study:
"GlaxoSmithKline: Sourcing Complex Professional Services" (N9-414-003)

Pharmaceutical company GlaxoSmithKline (GSK) uses an innovative approach to procuring outside legal counsel: it replaces relationship-based selection and law firms' traditional time-based billing with data-driven decision making and an online reverse auction. In the case, GSK is hit with a potentially devastating suit and must hire a firm in time to respond. The recently hired managing attorney, Sophia Keating, grapples with GSK's approach. The GSK veterans assure her that the approach drives down costs and improves the quality of work by systematically increasing the rigor in the procurement process. Still skeptical, Sophia runs the process of systematically analyzing and comparing the competing firms' bids. This case also describes the process by which these tools were created and adopted. Beyond the implications for law firms and other service providers, lessons from this case are applicable for teaching about institutional change, procurement processes relevant to many fields, and how to increase rigor in typically informal business processes.

(http://hbr.org/product/glaxosmithkline-sourcing-complex-professional-services/an/414003-PDF-ENG)

Research report: The state of legal procurement

Dr. Silvia Hodges Silverstein

Procurement's role in buying legal services keeps evolving. The three studies on the state of legal procurement that I conducted in 2011, 2012, and 2014, clearly demonstrate that procurement practices gain more and more influence on the category. In 2011, legal procurement was limited to a small number of very large companies, almost exclusively from the financial services sector and the pharmaceutical industry. Only three years later, many corporations turn to procurement for help in sourcing legal services. Fortune 500 corporations tend to employ their own legal procurement team while medium-sized companies hire consultants that organize legal procurement consortiums to achieve greater buying power. Here's what else I found:

Procurement gets more and more influence on the legal budget: In 2012, half of the respondents influenced less than 20% of the legal budget. The number has grown to 28% today. On the upper end, in

2012, only a small number (less than 10% of respondents), claimed to influence "over 90%" or "all" of the legal budget. This number rose to 25% in 2014. Keep in mind that a portion of legal spend may not be part of the legal budget, but be in the budget of different business unit stakeholders.

Procurement's role is that of the buyer, influencer, and gate keeper: Research shows that legal procurement does not decide which law firms will be chosen nor do they have the ability to veto a firm selection decision. The GC and the designated lawyers still retain these rights. CEOs and other top management are also typically not involved in the final decision about the law firms—unless it is for a matter of highest priority. CEOs care about the total cost and the win rate. They typically delegate a specific choice to the GC. Legal procurement's main role is that of a "buyer" and "influencer."

As buyers, legal procurement professionals are responsible for price and contract negotiation, as well as for the engagement letter, retainer or framework agreement. Legal and procurement often assume "good cop" and "bad cop" roles, relieving in-house counsel of the sometimes unpleasant price negotiations. As influencers, they aim to affect the outcome of a decision with their opinion. Legal procurement professionals are also "gatekeepers," they control the flow of information from the firm to the deciders. What they're not is "initiators" of sourcing legal service. In-house lawyers continue to indicate which legal services are needed.

Procurement professionals are well-educated: While lawyers often accuse legal procurement of lacking legal substance, ill-equipped to understand and buy legal services, we found that about one fifth of legal procurement professionals have a legal background. The remaining majority of respondents in the studies held MBA degrees or bachelor degrees in business subjects.

Procurement is moving into higher-value legal services: Procurement is typically involved in purchasing routine services, but has made progress in purchasing "bread and butter" legal services, those between high-stakes work and commodities. According to the 2014 study, procurement is increasingly involved in the purchasing of more complex, high-value, and high-stakes legal services. All types of matters have become subject to scrutiny, from litigation and transactional work to advisory work.

Procurement expects significant discounts: "You would not buy sticker price at the car dealer," remarked a legal procurement professional at a Fortune 100 company. Unless AFAs are used, legal procurement clearly expects discounts on law firm's hourly rates. Half of the respondents in the 2014 study expect a discount of over 20%. About a quarter of them expect a discount of over 25%. At the same time, they realize that unless they are able to control the number of hours spent on their matters and the level of time-keepers, discounts alone are not all that helpful.

Procurement's tools include negotiations, reverse auctions, and billing guidelines: Procurement typically gets involved with the negotiation of master service agreements (MSA), management of the panel selection or legal commodities such as eDiscovery. This is often done through so-called "reverse auctions." In a reverse auction, a client puts work out for bid online. Multiple firms compete with each other to offer the best price that meets all of the specifications of the bid. Standard practices include billing guidelines and a robust invoice review process as well as case management guidelines.

Legal procurement also conducts benchmarking analysis (71% of respondents), followed by rate increase analysis and invoice audits (67% each). Half of the respondents forecast budgets, followed by AFA analysis and key performance indicator analysis. Procurement also embraces legal spend management (75%) and eBilling (71%). Contract database, matter management and in-house eDiscovery are used by 40-50% of respondents in the survey. Firms' project management and process improvement capabilities are increasingly important: 48% of respondents in the survey deemed them "very important," another 16% as "important."

Billing guidelines are legal procurement's most common standard practice when sourcing legal services, used by 81% of respondents. It is good procurement practice to make the organization's terms and conditions (T&C) be part of the minimum requirements upfront. T&C should get accepted before an RFP is issued together with a Non-Disclosure Agreement (NDA). Attempts to deviate from the T&C typically count against the firm during the evaluation process. Also important are invoice review processes (70%). Case management and counsel selection and evaluation processes as well as analysis have gained in importance since the 2012 survey.

Procurement does some tire-kicking: How often do new suppliers win business over the incumbent law firms in an RFP issued by their organization? "Sometimes," says the majority (58%) of legal procurement professionals. "Often" say 25%; "Rarely" 17%. No-one answered "All the time" or "Never." Law firms need to carefully qualify opportunities and be clear their go/no-go criteria to avoid wasting their time and resources. Not every RFP should receive the same level of attention. Firms need to have a clear understanding of when they draw the line or when an "opportunity" is not one that they should be interested in. Only RFPs that are in line with the firm's strategy should be pursued.

What firms should do

It is worth speaking directly with the client to learn more about how procurement works in their organization, what influence procurement has, and how legal and procurement departments collaborate. Start building a relationship with the legal procurement. As a key stakeholder with growing influence, most procurement officers are open to learning more about what services firms currently provide and those the firm may be able to provide in the future. They may be looking for ways to consolidate spend, or to increase spend with the goal of getting volume discounts. Law firms should be aware of procurement's goals, objectives, challenges, and strategies.

Embrace the business side of the legal practice: Law firms also have to rethink how they market themselves, how they deliver and manage legal services: Procurement professionals demand predictability, project and budget management even more than most GCs. It is advisable to understand which metrics procurement uses when evaluating law firms. Procurement believes that if you know your business, you should know how long something takes and how much something should cost.

Understand what your client's procurement department wants and values: What convinces procurement the most is expertise in the matter at hand, experience with similar matters or "closest to the pin." Firms win points if they can demonstrate that they solved a similar issue for another client and can hit the ground running without needing to conduct extensive (expensive) research. Procurement also likes to see industry experience and a robust project management approach as they promise the efficiency procurement seeks. Procurement looks for compliance with AFAs and billing guidelines as well as past results. Responsiveness ("They are willing to help us to provide prompt service") was an important subjective factor that influences the law firm decision, followed by Reliability ("They are able to perform the service dependably and accurately") and Availability ("They are there when we need them").

Previous relationships with the organization, Chemistry ("We like working with them"), Empathy ("They make an effort to know our company and its needs"), and Assurance ("They have the required skills and knowledge to perform the service") were more important subjective factors than relationships with specific lawyers. Peer recommendations and industry rankings have little importance for legal procurement professionals. The (lowest) price, which was one of the two least important factors in the 2012 study, on the other hand, has gained in importance. Clients appear to be less shy about their intent to save cost.

When assessing firms' value adds, legal procurement see great value in Continued Legal Education (CLE) seminars and business-level training as well as free "hotline" access for quick questions or to discuss new matters. Other desired value-adds include: in-person visits of the client's office, plant, or facility to get to know their business; participation on internal calls that provide insight into a specific business or practice area; secondments; provision or development of basic templates and forms; conducting pre-matter planning sessions; and share-points with real-time access to the company's documents.

Procurement may not be the final decision-maker when it comes to legal services, but all three legal procurement studies suggest that firms are well advised to work with procurement, understand what is important to them as they represent the client at large, and to create a capability to respond to procurement demands. For law firms, this means get your cost in order, improve your efficiency and processes, and be ready to sharpen your pencil.

About the methodology: The 2014 study was conducted in Q1 2014. Links to the Qualtrics survey were posted to LinkedIn procurement groups and sent to a list of legal procurement professionals by email. 40% of respondents had the title procurement/sourcing manager, 32% chief procurement officer or director. The majority of respondents came from Fortune 500 companies. The 2011 study was conducted on Surveymonkey, the 2012 study on Qualtrics.

"I bought the law" – Outside counsel management

Lynn D. Krauss

Let me start this article by saying that I had written the first version of this article titled "I Bought The Law" back in 1999 for the annual conference of the Institute for Supply Management's conference. A lawyer by training, I had switched to procurement when my company, Dow Corning, turned to the legal department for help. After a few years in procurement, I returned to the legal department, where I am now Chief of Staff and oversee legal operations.

In some ways, little has changed and I didn't need to amend my initial article too much. Legal departments continue to be under pressure to cut costs and reduce outside expenses—just like other areas of their companies. Now, much has been written in the meantime about the convergence of legal work to fewer firms; the emergence of specialized temporary legal service providers; the unbundling of services; and the expanded alternative billing options, yet still few in-house attorneys have practical experience or expertise to maximize the return on their outside expenditures. Procurement on the other hand, brings skills, processes, discipline, and focus to complement the legal knowledge and experience of the in-house attorneys. The issue is that individual attorneys and/or legal management have long maintained the sole discretion in hiring outside counsel. So while top company management may encourage procurement's involvement, in-house lawyers may be reluctant to share responsibility for purchasing legal services.

Over time, procurement may earn an increasingly significant role in the acquisition of legal services by demonstrating to in-house attorneys the value they add to the legal service purchase process. For example, procurement may assist in-house attorneys with drafting balanced engagement agreements, defining the scope of projects, asking good questions, negotiating and structuring compensation and payment terms, evaluating supplier performance, and leveraging business with preferred suppliers—in essence, bringing familiar procurement disciplines to professional service purchases.

Procurement's techniques can be very useful for the legal department, so let me introduce you to trusted tactics for successful "supplier" management:

1. **Articulate objectives and scope.** Users of goods generally create written specifications to communicate their needs to the buyer and potential suppliers. While the practice of documenting specifications for goods is well ingrained within most organizations, the practice of documenting the scope and objectives for professional service projects may be foreign to in-house counsel and other internal service users. Procurement can help internal users clarify and communicate their needs to potential suppliers by asking relevant questions. How broad is the project? What are the goals, priorities, and desired results? What tasks need to be done? When and

where? What kind of knowledge and experience will be needed to accomplish these? How critical is cost and what is the range?

2. **Analyze make/buy decisions.** Once the scope and objectives for the project are documented. Procurement can encourage a make/buy analysis of individual tasks to determine which may be done better, faster or cheaper by using internal knowledge, skills, capabilities and/or existing work product. For example, procurement might ask in-house counsel whether the company has tried similar cases and whether it has existing research, briefs, etc. Or whether a particular task might be better performed by someone within the company who is familiar with the products, the company or its practices. The goal is to avoid re-inventing the wheel and to save the cost for others to re-invent them. Procurement can assure that the law department has taken stock of its acquired knowledge, skills, capabilities and work product. After the assessment, procurement and internal users will be in a better position to identify remaining gaps to be filled by external service providers.

3. **Select internal managing counsel and external lead counsel, then the team members.** Traditionally, in-house counsel selected the lead outside counsel to handle a project on a turn-key basis. As the project progressed, the lead counsel used others in his firm to assist as needed. New staff revolved in and out of the project, and considerable billable time and effort was expended bringing them up to speed on the specifics of the project. In addition, projects became training grounds for inexperienced associates who spent many billable hours re-inventing the wheel. This approach does not promote continuity, efficiency or cost-effectiveness. Traditional hourly billing methods provide no incentive to curb such inefficiencies; in fact, just the opposite.

4. **Selecting lead counsel remains the first step in establishing a cost-effective project team.** Rather than abdicating staffing responsibility to the lead counsel, the internal managing counsel together with the lead outside counsel should together identify the skills and experience necessary to perform various tasks and select team members based on their abilities to fill the needed roles and to work effectively with other team members. Membership need not be limited to those working for the lead counsel's firm. In-house staff, temporary service providers, and contract research specialists may round-out the project team. Tasks should be assigned to those who can complete them most effectively and cost-efficiently, taking advantage of existing knowledge, expertise and work product. Team membership should only change as mutually agreed upon to avoid costly re-education of new members.

5. **Define the win and the value.** Many outside counsel believe that every project deserves a "Cadillac" solution. They will leave no stone unturned, they will dot every "i," cross every "t," and make every argument that can be made up to the Supreme Court. They also will charge you for every stone turned, every "I" dotted, every "t" crossed, and every argument made. Sometimes this approach aligns with your needs. But if you prefer a more cost-conscious, focused approach, or if you want counsel to pursue alternative dispute resolution rather than litigation, you need to communicate your desires and reach agreement on objectives and strategies at the outset. For every objective, define an absolute minimum, desired result, and exceeded expectations, while also identifying the value of each.

6. **Structure compensation to reward results and efficiencies.** Include a budget with timing and milestones for payment. Compensation for attorneys, engineers and other professionals is frequently based on hourly billing. Hourly billing may work well if you

selected the right team members, each member is devoted to providing cost-effective service aligned with your objectives, and hourly rates are reasonable. Even so, your company would probably like to know approximately how much the project will cost and when payments will be due. Creating a budget with timing and milestones for payment helps assure that the project is well thought-out in advance. Many firms also will consider AFAs. Routine projects or large blocks of services may be placed with fixed fees that provide certainty to the company and incentives for efficiencies to the firm. Some companies negotiate bonuses for favorable results in exchange for discounts in hourly fees. Volume discounts in hourly fees may also be negotiated for large matters or multiple projects. Procurement professionals, skilled in exploring price options, can provide valuable assistance to internal users in structuring and negotiating compensation.

7. **Leverage knowledge, experience and work product.** To obtain cost-effective services, it is essential to leverage knowledge, experience and existing work product. Team members should be selected for their knowledge and expertise. Existing work product must be made easily available to team members. New knowledge should be shared among team members as appropriate. Newly developed work product including research, memos, briefs, etc. should be captured and shared for use on the project at hand, other contemporaneous projects and future projects.

8. **Put technology to work.** Email, teleconferencing, and web-based meeting technologies can facilitate timely and effective communication between team members. Document creation, storage and retrieval technologies enhance accessibility of previously developed work product. Electronic databases can power legal research and sharing. Docketing software can simplify scheduling challenges. If unused or poorly used, these tools are

expensive and unproductive. If embraced and effectively used by team members, technology can greatly improve communications, results and cost-effectiveness.

9. **Maintain open communication between team members.** Team members should keep in touch with one another as needed, communicating important developments on the project. Key decisions should be defined in advance and reviewed with lead counsel and the internal company contact before proceeding at specific milestones. Positive feedback is cheap and effective. Never pass up the opportunity to tell someone, "Well done."

10. **Evaluate performance and provide feedback.** Procurement may assist internal end-users in developing and implementing a supplier performance evaluation process, as it aligns with expectations, objectives, and results. By providing feedback to suppliers on their performance compared to your expectations and compared to the performance of other suppliers, you may improve areas of weakness and encourage them build upon their strengths. The process also helps narrow the field of suppliers with whom your company places future business.

11. **Standardize, aggregate, and leverage.** The process of aggregating and leveraging procurement power with fewer law firms across multiple projects is known as convergence. By working with fewer and better firms, companies create economies of scale, reduce learning curves, and make it easier to manage outside services. It becomes easier to negotiate discounted billing rates, fixed fees, or other alternative billing structures advantageous to the company and the firm.

The tactics I described may seem very familiar to procurement professionals, yet alien to in-house attorneys. Procurement's supplier management skills, processes, and discipline can complement the service-specific knowledge and experience of the internal professionals. Together, procurement and internal legal professionals can obtain the most cost-effective and valuable outside services. So let procurement have a seat at the table!

What legal procurement really wants

Andy Krebs

Sourcing professionals are often viewed as very tactical, short sighted, and focused solely on cost. I admit there are sourcing professionals that are focused solely on cost. They typically deal with highly repeatable events, perhaps driven by the nature of the commodity or their particular skill set. Unfortunately this "cost is king" persona is painted across the profession with a wide brush. From my experience, highly talented sourcing experts who focus on the overall outcome, the effects on the corporation, and how their actions shape the landscape of the industry are closer to reality. These professionals are driven by the desire to create a competitive advantage for the legal team and their employer.

Allow me to shed some light on who we—procurement professionals— are, why we want to be involved, and where we can add value. Legal procurement professionals strive to be the trusted advisor of the legal department, one who listens, collaborates, and provides knowledge and insight. We understand that we can advise the legal team, but the choice is ultimately theirs.

Procurement continues to gain credibility and confidence utilizing the knowledge garnered in other professional services areas. Procurement professionals bring their value-added or competitive advantage to the legal department by tapping into their skill set, knowledge, and business acumen. Increasing, they are becoming trusted advisors to the legal department, seen as someone who enables the solution rather than providing one. This is possible through hard work, perseverance, and partnering with the legal department. It takes time to influence a very integral part of the organization that often faces "bet the company" concerns and did not want to be hindered by procurement.

Procurement professionals can add value to many parts of the process: RFPs, supplier management, market analysis, supplier negotiations, and an unbiased, structured process. Our goal is make the process, selection, and supplier management as easy as possible for our colleagues in the legal department. Let me discuss RFPs and supplier management.

RFPs are a necessary evil in any spend area. They enable decision makers to view different ideas and strategies on how to resolve the issue at hand. Procurement helps legal to professionally manage the RFP event and ensures an even playing field for all participants. The idea that an RFP outcome has already been pre-determined prior to the event is simply not true. Procurement professionals strive to have the competition open to the best-suited partners, ensuring the best ideas and strategies are brought to the table. Procurement professionals work with the legal team to identify the best candidates to match the given requirements. If we identify other suitable candidates through our market research and industry ties, we recommend them. However, legal has the final say about that.

The RFP process can take many different paths depending on the scope and situation. It can range from procurement as the single point of contact or as an advisor (if legal is running the RFP). Procurement is involved to ensure the RFP's integrity. Legal and procurement develop the scope of work that each participant will review and submit the RFP. They then work on a scoring matrix based on the requirements of the RFP. The scoring matrix ensures that the choice is defendable, explaining how/why a particular firm was selected. In a next step, the team reviews the firms' RFP responses and scores them. If firms participate in the RFP that have never worked for the organization, procurement may ask them to go through a financial and risk assessment to eliminate possible surprises. Armed with all the information, the team decides to shortlist the suppliers and has them present in a beauty contest—it will simply move towards a decision.

Procurement typically sends a notice to advise firms of the organization's decision and may give information as to why a firm was not selected. I encourage our teams to also offer a 30-minute post-mortem call if the supplier chooses to request one. This is done to provide closure for the supplier and to provide insight as to why they were not selected. It will show weak areas as well as areas they did great in. The idea behind it is to enable firms to have a stronger response in their next RFP. Contrary to common belief, we want firms to succeed. This helps keep the market fresh with ideas and keeps it from getting stale.

Here are some do's and don'ts for winning an RFP when sourcing is involved:

Do's	Don'ts
It is OK to say "No" (you don't need to participate in every RFP)	No circumventing the process
Ask clarifying questions or ask for a Q&A meeting	No responding if not capable to perform the work
Respond to the RFP exactly how they ask	Not following the requested template/process
Respond on time	No late submissions
Provide alternatives/a la carte	No canned presentations
Offer AFAs	Not asking questions
Outline any efficiencies identified	Negative campaign against peers
Think of all the business, financial, and operation considerations that they may not have adequately addressed (for their business, not yours as a vendor!)	
Read the RFP introduction and background sections with great care	
Craft a set of account-specific questions that focus on the 'why' as well as the 'what/how': • *Detailed:* ask all the 'how's'… but no meaningless questions • *Gap-exposing:* identify requirements that should have been included based on the stated objectives but are missing • *Comprehensive:* address all aspects of the RFP with your insightful questions • *Insightful:* ask probing questions • *Relevant:* tie requested capabilities to business value	

Supplier management is another key component where procurement can add value to the legal department. I am not talking about the day-to-day management of the relationship, but the feedback loop. Just like it takes a lot of resources to win a new account for a firm, it takes a lot of resources for companies to switch suppliers when the incumbent firms are not providing the value you expected from them. It is imperative to provide the firms with an avenue for feedback and push for continuous improvement. Please bare in mind that we want you to do well: it does not serve us well if you are no longer in business.

We can provide feedback in different ways. I like surveys for our legal team and anyone relevant that interfaces with them. The legal team and I outline the key areas to judge the firms on. We then take the feedback, trend them against past results, trend against their peers, and then provide them the information in a face-to-face meeting or via telephone. I have had great success with this process: one of our firms was performing below its peers, but after a face-to-face meeting during which we provided all the data and comments, they made some drastic changes. They truly took the feedback to heart and went from "worst to first" in less than six months. What's more, not only did we notice the change, but so did all their clients. The firm still thanks us just about every time we are on the phone with them!

Research report: Bridging the gap between legal & procurement

Brian Lee

In their cost control efforts, many GCs focused on reducing the fees paid to outside counsel. This was not surprising given that outside counsel spending accounted for more than half of a typical legal department's budget according to the CEB 2013 Legal Budget Diagnostic. Advances in eBilling and matter management technologies made it easier for companies not only to track their expenses, but control law firm spending. Nevertheless, legal departments often dismiss procurement's ability to add value in sourcing legal services. Making matters worse, procurement finds legal departments reluctant to cede control over their spending, and believe that lawyers overemphasize their relationships with law firms and the custom nature of the work performed. Recognizing this inherent tension, CEB analyzed how legal departments work with procurement departments in sourcing and evaluating outside counsel. The following list summarizes key recommendations CEB developed in conducting this research.

Build a collegial relationship: Law firm selection can be a touchy point of conversation for lawyers who often choose law firms based on prior personal and working relationships. Legal and procurement departments must build trust and establish mutual objectives to lay the foundation for a successful partnership. One way to do this is to start with an agreed upon set of objectives and responsibilities to allay any concerns the legal department may have about losing control of the selection process.

Create opportunities for procurement to show additional value: Legal departments often do not involve procurement when sourcing law firms because they believe that procurement is only focused on saving money. Procurement, however, can often show value in other ways: they can track matter outcomes or in-house evaluations to lend an empirical lens to sourcing law firms. A more holistic view that incorporates cost (but does not rely solely upon it) would increase the likelihood of an effective partnership (and outcome) when making law firm selection decisions.

Institutionalize the partnership through the creation of a mixed team: Prior to partnering, the legal and procurement departments should create a team that manages and oversees the collaborative effort, preferably with executive support. This group should be led by a project manager that could serve as a mediator between the departments should issues arise, and could provide a useful joint resource during the selection process.

Test the partnership: To overcome key objections, the legal and procurement departments should conduct a non-binding test phase prior to establishing a fixed framework defining the partnership. During this period, aspects of the partnership can be adjusted to uncover roadblocks, surface unspoken assumptions, and ensure that the roles of each department are clearly defined.

Establish a clear partnership framework: The legal and procurement departments should meet to discuss the framework for their sourcing partnership, identify specific roles, and set expectations. The legal department may choose to use the initial meeting to educate the procurement function about its selection criteria for outside counsel. Additionally, legal may choose to create a roster of preferred vendors for each matter type, which procurement could then use to disseminate RFPs.

Identify and harness core strengths: The different strengths legal and procurement possess can, when combined, yield valuable benefits, provided that the two functions identify and accept the unique abilities of the other. CEB recommends using procurement's expertise in areas such as negotiation and outside counsel performance management, and using legal's expertise in the classification of legal services and type of work. Legal should also identify the routine matters where legal service is more fungible for procurement to play a larger role.

Build flexibility into sourcing initiatives: Legal departments should have the ability to make a final determination of the law firm used, with procurement having narrowed down the number of qualified law firms for a particular matter based on hourly rate, prior experience, and internal evaluations. Legal then chooses between these firms to ensure proper fit. This will allow legal departments to feel empowered and be ultimately more cooperative.

Challenges and benefits of a closer procurement/legal partnership: A close procurement/legal partnership is rare in most companies. Previous research such as the CEB Legal Department Transformation Diagnostic Survey shows that legal constitutes the function least served by procurement support. This likely stems from many legal departments' views that procurement's handling of outside counsel selection is of high risk (and low value) to them. In addition, a recent CEB survey of business partners on their perception of procurement shows that legal departments are skeptical of their value.

While legal departments acknowledge the importance of procurement departments in general, they believe that procurement is less effective in their role specific to legal's needs. The gap between legal departments' view of the importance of procurement and their effectiveness is among the highest of any corporate function. This suggests a notable dissatisfaction in the use of procurement in sourcing law firms.

A closer look at this skepticism reveals that legal departments refrain from instituting a closer relationship with procurement because they weigh heavily the relationships that they build with outside counsel, a traditionally immeasurable factor. However, if carefully managed, both sides can benefit from the other function's strengths. The following table highlights common challenges and benefits of legal/procurement cooperation:

Challenge	Benefit
Quantification of legal services Each legal matter is considered distinct and impossible to standardize, creating different approaches from procurement and legal.	*Reduced administrative burden* Procurement helps legal realize cost savings without having to actively manage law firms.
Lack of expertise on legal matters Procurement struggles to differentiate between the types of tasks and services legal requires.	*Improved negotiation potential* The partnership benefit from procurement's negotiation experience allows the two functions to achieve better outcomes.
Lack of business understanding Procurement believes legal has little insight into business priorities.	*Internal evaluation of sourcing process* Procurement staff act as 'internal consultants' and provide unbiased

	analytics on processes within the legal department.
Inadequate metrics While procurement focuses on saving money, legal recognizes that the lowest billable hour does not necessarily equate to the best legal service or highest ROI.	*Enhanced law firm performance management procedures* Procurement crafts standardized performance management procedures, the outcomes of which inform future sourcing initiatives.
Distinct system of internal controls Procurement worries about legal's apparent lack of formal agreements in place to protect the company's interests and confidential information.	*Ability to harness strengths* By allowing procurement to handle commoditized items, RFPs, and other routine work, legal can focus on higher value work.

Procurement & pricing: The benefits of partnering

Steven Manton

Companies are seeking greater value for their legal spend and complete transparency on costs. While law firms are making solid strides to adapt to meet this need, there is still a gap in what companies want and what law firms are providing in response. One only has to look at the path to success in both the corporate and legal environments to see how this divergence arises.

Law students succeed by competing against their fellow students for the top grades, they promote their individual attributes to get accepted into the best law firms, and on arrival work hard to prove they have what it takes to become a partner. Within most law firms, individual partners work diligently to build a book of business, which in-turn, determines what they bring home after a hard day's grind.

Top management at most Fortune 500 companies has studied business. To succeed in their MBA programs, they had to collaborate in teams to complete assignments. Their companies succeed by leveraging service offerings and product placements through internal cross-functional teams and multi-disciplined research and development. When CEOs look to their legal department and outside counsel, they are often mystified by the close law firm/legal department relationship and frustrated with the general sense of low value compared to significant legal spend. Many legal departments lack an accurate way to measure quality of service, the potential cost savings achievable through risk avoidance or early settlement, as well as other potential service quality attributes. Top management's frustration with increasing legal spend, coupled with difficulty in measuring return on investment in economic uncertainty, led to a mandate to apply "normal" corporate procurement techniques to purchasing legal services.

Pricing experts: financially astute and business-minded like procurement professionals. In response to the increased scrutiny on price and efficiency, law firms have hired pricing and legal project management experts to help them navigate the new demands. Like procurement professionals, legal business professionals are financially astute and commercially orientated and trained to focus on the business side of the law. While it is difficult to predict what role these new functions will play in the future, there is plenty of evidence that business professionals will play a greater and more influential part in developing strong relationships with procurement. John Ferko, executive vice president at Miles & Stockbridge observed that "for nearly a decade now I have been reading about the legal industry shifting to using experts for client relationship management. While other professional service sectors have embraced the concept and reaped the rewards, the legal industry has resisted such change. What we are seeing now with pricing and legal project professionals working directly with procurement and legal department business folks, could be the first real concrete shift in how corporations and law firms develop long lasting and stronger relationships."

Purvi Sanghvi, director of strategic pricing at Paul Hastings, said that "law firm and in-house business professionals speak the same language, understand the numbers, and can see through the operational issues to act as effective conduits between the in-house counsel and the law firm partner." The real value of the procurement/pricing business relationships is derived through collaboration. Paul Roy, senior director, finance and administration for the legal department at Time Warner noticed "when speaking directly with a law firm partner about billings, they are getting their information from someone who is really my counterpart in the law firm, a billing specialist. When dealing directly with a billing specialist I can resolve issues more quickly and easily."

Within a few weeks of arrival at my current firm, I was leading the negotiations with the procurement department of one of our top clients to help them navigate through the process. Having the ability to keep personal relationships out of the price negotiation sandbox helped remove emotions from the negotiations and allowed for a smoother and more structured discussion. With many large corporations now working with procurement, it has become increasingly common for the in-house function to directly request that the law firm pricing professional be involved in the relationship discussion. Justin Ergler, director of alternative fee intelligence and analytics within the Global External Legal Relations Department at GlaxoSmithKline "asks that the law firm partner work with their pricing folks on all significant matters; I just know that the budget will be better thought through and that I can work with them (pricing) directly to iron out any aspects that need refinement."

Where the collaboration between these business professionals generates added value is not necessarily when things are going well, but often when relationship expectations are not aligned. Julie Lee, legal program manager at eBay faced a situation where the law firm partner was technically brilliant but not effective in managing the workflow. Her team felt there were inefficiencies that could be resolved, but knowing the personality of the partner, they knew it would be a challenge to deliver the message without causing offense: "Developing the relationship was instrumental and we were able to talk openly with the law firm's pricing person to explain what we were seeing and we collaborated to reach an outcome that really worked." Julie noted that her organization "received the high level of technical guidance we were after and the law firm was able to find support to help the partner control the staffing inefficiencies; it was a win/win that bolstered the relationship." These relationships become even more prominent when defining, measuring, and rewarding "value." The metrics included rates and costs as well as soft factors such as training, knowledge management, secondees, and level of service.

The associate GC of a leading financial institutions company appreciated the input from experts within law firms on KM systems and practice technology, keeping them abreast of useful new software tools for their large legal department. Collaborating on providing training to their attorneys was also noted as a substantial added value, especially on legal changes that directly affected their business units. Much of this was achieved by connecting their law firms' operational experts through "account managers." He wondered, however that "law firms have not been pushing their operations people more forward in their interactions. This represents a wasted opportunity as more interaction would greatly assist him in managing the needs of the legal department."

The importance of not only delivering first-rate legal product, but also closer operational alignment, continues to become more critical. Jerome Posatko, head of finance for the legal department at The Carlyle Group suggested to "let the lawyers spend their time focusing on the legal issues and we, the operational professionals, can deal with the logistics; relationships truly benefit from this approach." Carlyle continually evaluates its use of global outside counsel to maintain a right-sized list of providers, and while Jerome does not always make the final decision on which law firm to be used, he clearly influences preferences based on both quantitative analysis and qualitative perception of value, including firms' ability and willingness to maintain open lines of communication, explore other ideas and get creative.

A word of caution: Having spent several years consulting on procurement for Accenture, Barry Mehew, global director of pricing strategy and legal project management at Mayer Brown, however, warned that "procurement does not differentiate between the type of the legal services they go after–they are directly incentivized to generate savings and while there may be some low hanging fruit and the need to continue to demonstrate their value, they specifically adopt a strategy of focusing on any one particular area of legal services. Law firms need to put the right business people around the table with a client's procurement team to enhance communications and enable a greater understanding of what is meant by client value and expectations." Pier D'Angelo, chief pricing and practice officer at Australia's Allens observed that when the in-house department reports up to the CEO on value, the discussion inevitably focuses on the level of discount. Rarely are other factors such as risk mitigation or a successful acquisition that supports strategic aspirations raised. "I often say they are reporting on price but asking us about value; we need to align more and collaborate to help you deliver the right message to the company board."

Procurement & outside counsel: The benefits of partnering

Colleen F. Nihill

Merriam-Webster defines "partnership" as a relationship that, "usually involv[es] close cooperation between parties having specified and joint rights and responsibilities." Many times, however, the relationships between clients and law firms do not progress in such a collaborative manner. Instead, communications between them can seem downright unfriendly and adversarial with both sides trying to gain the best bargaining advantage over one another. The very definition of the "partnership," however, offers guidance on how this dynamic can be changed: through close cooperation with regular communication and specified, joint rights and responsibilities between procurement and outside counsel.

This type of teamwork must be exercised in connection with key decision points during the legal engagement lifecycle: Risk assessment, negotiation, budget preparation, and relationship review.

Risk assessment: Many companies regularly undergo internal risk assessments to mitigate issues that could adversely affect corporate performance (e.g. regulatory, reputational, human resources-related, technology-related issues). Procurement departments often formally request law firms to partner with them to help identify both business and legal risks. Examples are evidenced in RFPs, preferred provider policies, which ask for greater law firm input and outside counsel manuals which request assistance in the development of a risk assessments before, during and upon the conclusion of a legal engagement. To appropriately respond to these inquiries, law firms must understand the business and the culture of the client. This type of understanding cannot be established through the response process alone. For the law firm to add valuable input, discussions about the company's business objectives must be had long before the release of a RFI or RFP and be focused on the company's short term and long term strategic goals. Both parties must be responsible for initiating this dialogue. Partnering on risk assessment benefits both procurement and outside counsel by:

- Identifying potential risks and constraints to set reasonable expectations;
- Providing an action plan for unforeseen events;
- Identifying impact of successful and unsuccessful results;
- Providing a foundation for better future decision making.

Negotiation: Just as legal departments have begun to embrace procurement, so too have firms increased the hiring of business professionals steeped in disciplines such as financial analysis and project management. The inclusion of these individuals alone, however, will not in and of itself optimize either party's position. The process itself must change: First, the negotiation process must begin long before a specific opportunity arises. Best practices would suggest that in-house teams speak regularly with their existing roster of counsel as well as specialists in areas where they anticipate needs. Second, an open line of communication with outside counsel during the negotiation process must be established to allow the firm to learn as much as they can about the client's legal and financial objectives. Accordingly, the negotiation discussions should not just center around the financial arrangement, but include healthy dialogue around the delivery of the legal service, such as a summary of the project objectives, scope of work, key members of the legal team, a communication schedule, provisions for change requests, as well as feedback mechanisms and timing. Partnering during negotiation benefits procurement and outside counsel by:

- Defining business goals and objectives which better inform legal strategy;
- Establishing the scope of work, key deliverables, timeline expected results;
- Guiding the legal team composition and resource requirements;
- Setting fee arrangements that reflect value and encourage a trusted relationship.

Budget preparation: If designed correctly, a budget should reflect the costs associated with a legal engagement as well as type of fee arrangement that best encompasses the company's cost management rationale. Most importantly, a budget should reflect the client's strategic business objectives. Poorly designed budgets do not take into account the business problem the client is trying to solve. Understanding whether a client is interested in a litigation strategy which favors early case settlement versus engaging in a protracted discovery period to strengthen its position is important for correctly developing the team composition and projecting the time frames for each phase of the matter. Taking into account the strategic objectives has the benefit of allowing the budget to become the basis of a detailed project plan which both parties can routinely refer to during the course of the engagement. Partnering during budgeting preparation benefits procurement and outside counsel by:

- Aligning price with case strategy and original assumptions;
- Providing in-house counsel with cost predictability measures to control costs;
- Fostering collaboration and communication by documenting assumptions and expected results;
- Allowing in-house counsel to better evaluate and manage company's legal spend.

Relationship review: Delivering constructive feedback can be very hard and developing a corrective course of action is often even harder. To avoid surprises and to properly assess the relationship, relationship scorecards that include quantitative and qualitative metrics should be used. It is critical to identify and solve problems immediately. Don't wait, but conduct relationship post-mortem on projects in addition to a general performance review. Partnering during relationship review benefits procurement and outside counsel by:

- Evaluating performance during the course of engagements;
- Identifying positive results and gaps at the end of engagements or key milestones;
- Allowing in-house counsel to evaluate law firms on metrics that support the company's goals;
- Streamlining data to compare firm performance and determine future legal spend.

Achieving value through sensible collaboration

Susan O'Brien

When the GC of a UK-based industrial operations company was asked to deliver cost savings against unpredictable events within the global legal department, he faced difficult decisions: With a multinational presence supporting operations for power plants and mass transit systems, he was wary of economizing at the expense of increased business risks. As he had to find at least one area of legal activity where the application of cost-cutting measures made sense and resulted in real impact to the company's bottom line, he focused on employment issues. He realized that it would take a large investment to bring the management of all these issues in-house, yet he wanted the services provided by numerous law firms done in a way that matched the knowledge and memory typical of inside counsel. He believed that incentivizing the firms to develop an insider's concern would likely be ineffectual.

Fortunately, his company operated in a culture of interdepartmental collaboration and trust. The legal team regularly partnered with stakeholders and had a high regard for procurement based on previous work where procurement had demonstrated great value in other business projects. The GC was confident that procurement had the necessary discipline, tools, and process knowledge to assist with a major employment law outsourcing initiative, even if the individuals were not subject matter experts in all aspects of legal operations.

The process began by defining the ideal outcome and envisioning ways to track success over time. The legal department wanted to work with a single global firm that was invested in the success of the company. The partnership had to be embedded, with individual lawyers demonstrating they were acting in the best interests of the company at all times. At the core was the legal department's desire to improve overall site compliance to the company's standard set of HR policies. They regarded this as the ultimate validation that onboarding a single firm—as opposed to investing in specialized in-house counsel—provided the greatest benefits and risk reduction. Given the huge degree of variability in the past, the legal department wanted a consistent approach to employment matters globally.

Search and selection: The team collaborated to arrive at a joint set of requirements. Contenders had to be well known for their robust multi-national employment practice in each of the company's operating locations and headquartered in the U.S. or the UK. Together, the team analyzed the company's annual payouts to firms by country, the number of calls for advice to outside counsel, and the percentage of issues resolved by the firms in favor of the company. As a result of their research, 25 firms were identified to participate in a formal RFP. The RFP included thought-provoking questions designed to give each firm an opportunity to expound on its business intelligence. The final document was issued in accordance with standard sourcing practices.

Procurement brought neutrality to the process, acting as a shield between the attorneys and law firm personnel. Their role as the "bad cop" was vital to successful negotiations. Their questions made the law firms rethink their rates and underlying assumptions about how the services would be delivered.

Although the process allowed the team to compare responses in terms of geography, fees, reputation, and staffing, it wasn't as easy to score the value-added services. These included criteria such as training, unique specialties, secure portals, online case management tools, and operational transparency. Evaluating partnership potential was also tricky: the best proposals exposed the maturity of the respondent's relationship management model. Due to the nature of the work, the GC desired a trusted partnership between the parties. It was important to provide early access to the company's operational plans without feeling the need to look over their shoulders.

In evaluating proposals, reviewers focused on responses that they believed would result in mutual rewards and long-term profitability. Projected cost savings, a key assessment element, was estimated through fee transparency and market pricing. Scope of services was clearly articulated to enable value comparisons. In some cases, firms were asked to open their books and validate the assumptions behind proposed AFAs. As a result, the final round of negotiations was amongst firms that demonstrated a real desire for the partnership and a willingness to share financial risks.

Tracking success: One firm emerged with all the desired qualifications. It bested the competition by offering a wide scope of services, a hotline for free (albeit time-restricted) advice, and substantially discounted fees. The agreement was structured as a "collared" fixed fee retainer with percentage triggers to manage financial risks: if the company's annual global demand for services were to exceed 10% of the projected work defined in the agreement, the firm would receive an additional payout. Similarly, if the volume of work were to fall below the 10% collar, the company would receive a rebate. This arrangement met the GC's goal for budget predictability and stability despite constraints imposed by unforeseen events.

In the years since this arrangement was executed, both parties still laud it as hugely successful. The law firm acknowledged that it was able to cross-sell other legal services not covered in the retainer and the company was able to maintain a strong position of leverage throughout each annual rate change process. Most importantly, the company maintained an overall sense that the employment portion of their legal duties was under control. The legal sourcing process itself remains embedded in the legal department's culture, and the company has since followed the same process to partner with firms doing immigration work and intellectual property law. In addition to claiming financial valuations each year since the sourcing event, compliance to policies has improved and new standardized processes have been deployed more efficiently across the globe.

A primer on reducing outside counsel spend

Susan O'Brien

Making an impact on legal spend can be the challenge of a procurement professional's career. They find themselves dealing with in-house attorneys who express an interest in reducing costs but face no repercussions when authorizing sizable payments in the pursuit of successful outcomes. They also encounter skepticism about standard sourcing practices because of the belief that lower outside counsel fees equate to inferior advice and services. However, with perseverance, solid strategies, and patience, procurement managers can become trusted partners among their legal peers. They can create a team that delivers better outside legal services and generates substantial savings for their organization.

Legal sourcing is not a one-time event or project. Complete collaboration means full adoption of the practices by legal and procurement's involvement at the initiation of all major matters. By letting lawyers focus on legal issues, procurement becomes a valued partner, and the company is ensured that the right practices are being followed to get the highest quality of services at the best prices. Over time, leadership roles will emerge, with procurement likely heading up much of the business relationship and negotiations, and legal teammates providing business intelligence and engagement feedback. Here are tips for approaching the legal category:

Overcome (negative) perceptions: The value of procurement lies in the premise that their involvement will let lawyers spend more time on legal issues and strategy. But gaining their trust can be a hard-fought battle. Procurement professionals have to overcome the perception of being outsiders who are ill-suited to the task of talking to prominent attorneys at prestigious firms. Without legal operations training, they may find it difficult to converse about "costs per phase of litigation" or "value adjusted fee arrangements." Some legal colleagues may assert competitive bid tendering adds too much time to the decision process, while others may be concerned about forfeiting their influence to select the firm or attorney handling their matters.

Any procurement manager stepping into this domain for the first time should be aware of these potential obstacles and confront the perceptions immediately by demonstrating proficiency in the legal operations of the company and speaking the language of lawyers. This requires focused dedication to the profession such as familiarity with law firm rankings, attendance at legal industry events, and active participation in legal procurement peer groups. Equally important are personal characteristics of flexibility, innovation, logic, persuasion, and demonstrating a sense of urgency in the completion of tasks.

Having an executive sponsor who embraces the concept of building a legal sourcing practice diminishes these misconceptions. GCs are the best champions since they are in a position to not only mandate cost reduction objectives for staff attorneys, but also facilitate procurement's access to their domain (e.g. eBilling and matter management systems). Depending on how legal is structured, procurement may choose to focus on a single practice area or business unit as the first point of ingress. Building a team that includes legal colleagues who are committed to cost reduction goals and functionally aligned to the executive sponsor will increase the chances of earning trust early in the process.

Take a practical approach: Developing a legal sourcing strategy begins with building a database of payment information. Deciphering the details may be challenging, but the numbers are likely to reveal non-relevant items like publication subscriptions, membership fees, training, and temporary labor. Specialized legal services, such as lobbying or tax advice, may be better re-categorized as "consultancy" services to be sourced through a non-legal work stream. Settlements are also generally out of scope since payouts cannot be influenced by procurement practices, although understanding and reporting trends may be of interest to the GC. Opinions will vary on which expenditures should be in scope for the first legal cost reduction initiative.

It is procurement's role to uncover patterns and opportunities buried in the data. For example, instead of dismissing patent fees as "out of scope" for cost saving efforts, the team may consider recommending specialized attorneys and engineers to investigate ways for the company to reduce the number of patent renewals. A seasoned procurement professional will not just ask questions, but listen carefully to ensuing discussions before attempting to identify the "right" spend. This body of payout information, scrubbed and vetted, will become the baseline from which cost reductions will be measured.

Conduct spend analysis: Most procurement managers have excellent analytic skills which are critical to developing sourcing strategies. Common break-outs for legal spend include:

- the number of firms actively engaged
- the number of new firms added annually
- payouts for eDiscovery charges, firm expenses or other disbursements
- office locations
- practice categories, such as HR advice, litigations, or patent law

With time and effort, the team will be able to cull out non-recurring costs such as local counsel engagements, expert witnesses, and co-defendant arrangements. Parsing the data in multiple ways will yield patterns and a better understanding of what costs can be affected by specialized sourcing practices.

Plan the projects, set the target: Organizations are often uncomfortable agreeing to cost reduction goals on unbudgeted, unplanned legal actions. Many well-intended legal sourcing projects stall at this point. Opportunities for savings increase with the number of work streams in the plan, billing system sophistication, and the department's appetite for process change. In many cases, legal departments lacking spend control behaviors can expect to achieve 10-30% cost reductions off the baseline spend, especially if they incorporate demand management and budget oversight practices. Achieving savings of this magnitude requires strong procurement/legal collaboration and executive-mandated objectives.

Once legal colleagues are comfortable with the project goals, there are a number of practices that can make an impact on reducing outside counsel spend:

Billing guidelines and engagement letters: Lower costs and better service values can be achieved from clear communications of assumptions and expectations. Issuing a document that establishes the company's preferred terms is a basic tenet of any professional services engagement. Yet this discipline is often overlooked in the haste of engaging outside counsel when procurement is not involved. Something as simple as constructing good billing guidelines and sending them to firms at the onset of a new engagement can result in a powerful spend control tool that costs next to nothing to implement. At a minimum, the document should detail the legal department's expectations for matter staffing, reporting frequency, and billing practices. Incorporating prevailing engagement terms will help the team add relevant content. For example, until 2008 it was common practice for companies to reimburse firms for telephone, fax, and online legal research subscriptions, such as Westlaw or LexisNexis.

Today these are viewed as overhead expenses to be borne by the firm. The communication of expense policies can result in significant cost cutting for travel, overtime, and ad-hoc charges. The key to making the document effective is ensuring it is sent to all current and new firms. A letter or email from the GC with a request of acknowledgement is recommended. Procurement can provide value by tracking the responses and gaining further insight into the number and types of firms used.

Engagement letters detailing specific fee agreements and negotiated revisions to the billing guidelines are also essential. Having templates for every type of fee arrangement will standardize the practice of completing one letter for each new matter and ensuring its execution. The letters, along with the guidelines, provide a complete description of the behavior and budget expectations for both parties. They are critically important when engaging in AFAs to reduce the likelihood of misunderstandings.

Matter management and eBilling systems: With oversight from procurement and legal operations, eBilling enables more efficient invoice reviews and ensures that the company's engagement terms are applied consistently to all firms. System features can promote good invoicing practices and result in fewer charge disputes when used in conjunction with billing guidelines and engagement letters. If the guidelines establish parameters for meeting attendance and the eBilling tool is configured to set alerts for more than one meeting participant, the law firm is more likely to redact bills with multiple lawyers billing for one activity. If the engagement letter describes a procedure for changing or adding staff, eBilling systems can flag unidentified billers.

As a result, unapproved timekeepers are less likely to appear on invoices. Other benefits of linking the content of the guidelines to eBilling are budget and timekeeper rate change controls. Even the least sophisticated system is usually capable of highlighting duplicate billing entries or expenses that exceed maximum caps. Alert configurations can help speed up the review and approval time, resulting in a higher percentage of on-time payments. When set up to accept Legal Electronic Data Exchange Standard (LEDES) or Uniform Task Based Management System (UTBMS) codes, matter management and eBilling systems facilitate an accurate analysis of the costs of tasks across all matters and geographies. This information may give procurement and legal the confidence they need to negotiate alternative fees.

Competitive bidding: Arguing that it's the outcome that counts, not the fees, in-house attorneys are often uncomfortable with competitive bidding and block procurement from the firm selection decisions. Surely, success in legal matters is highly dependent on the unique knowledge and experience of the attorney, yet there is so much that can be gained from soliciting proposals when the tender is conducted in a manner supportive of the demands and deadlines of legal departments. In a bidding process, procurement should consider costs as a function of the matter dimensions. A number of issues could impact the comparison of costs among competitive bidders, including the complexity of the case or the attorney's experience with the judge or opposing counsel.

Typically, in-house attorneys will select which firms to invite to the bidding. However, procurement should develop their own insight into the legal market. Throughout the year, they can initiate and facilitate firm visits and presentations to increase the law department's exposure to respected and experienced attorneys from many practice areas. They can also solicit feedback and raise awareness of good results from less-well-known firms. RFPs should be constructed to elicit responses that not only check for conflicts, highlight experience, and enable rate comparisons, but provide insight into how a firm manages client relationships and provides value. This may include the transfer of knowledge, access to a firm's library of information, free CLE programs or other benefits.

Armed with market data, procurement can lead negotiations resulting in lower hourly fees, volume discounts, lower-cost staff locations, and fees tied to matter outcomes. Gaining cost savings can be a hard-won battle when there is attorney predisposition to use a particular firm. To balance bias, procurement should reference their previous spend analyses and know the average fees charged by similar attorneys based on years of experience, practice area, size of the firm, and firm location. While this information may not initially be viewed as relevant, the practice of incorporating data into the firm selection process will, over time, achieve the goal of bringing high-end firm rates closer to market averages. In the end, the lowest cost firm may not be chosen, but cost savings calculated from "first-to-final" proposals are still reportable benefits in most organizations.

Budgeting: Regardless of the fee arrangements established through an RFP, budget monitoring is an important component of a legal cost reduction strategy. While almost every other company expenditure has to be reviewed and approved, legal often gets a pass when asked, "How much will that legal action cost?" Using RFP responses, in-house attorneys should be requested to estimate total expenditures for matters anticipated to exceed a minimum threshold. This way, a budget can be established before the final round of negotiations and monitored by both parties. Budgets can also be tied to the eBilling platform to prevent overpayments. For AFAs, establishing a budget may also serve as the basis for fee caps, litigation phase payments, or incentive payments to firms.

AFAs: For AFAs to work, firms expect to be rewarded for efficiencies and law departments want to feel that they paid the right price to the right firm and achieved the right outcome. Opinions differ on why AFAs aren't always embraced, but the difficulty of measuring the savings or losses associated with complicated fee structures might be a factor. Billing arrangements alone do not lead to lower costs, which is why AFAs should be part of a larger strategy to develop partnerships with firms that commit to the success of the company. Legal procurement needs access to good baseline spend data and applied intelligence in order to assess AFA savings. Some questions that should be considered in the final assessment of the AFA value include: Did the company experience a better quality of service for the cost compared to similar issues in the past? Did the firm's attorney apply creative and successful strategies leading to faster resolution of the matter? Will the case resolution prevent the occurrence of similar issues, saving millions in additional legal fees? Was knowledge transferred to inside counsel so there will be less need for outside advice going forward?

Sustain the gains: The experience procurement acquires over time can lead to greater sophistication in the management of legal expenditures. Regardless of initial achievements gained using any of the approaches described above, maintaining a disciplined sourcing practice is essential to effectuating real value in the long run. An atmosphere of collaboration and trust is equally important to any one cost-control practice, and will ultimately be the real measurement of a successful legal sourcing practice.

Choosing preferred suppliers abroad

Dr. Ute Rajathurai

A Japanese proverb says, "Those who wish to do great things must take care of the small things first." This applies to clients seeking law firms as preferred suppliers as well as law firms seeking to be such preferred suppliers. We used this principle in every step of the process—from preparing and issuing the RFP, analysis of the firms' responses, the personal visit, to making the final decision—when selecting law firms in Japan.

The better the preparation, the more relevant and specific the RFP. We learned that the more specific the RFP, the more easily comparable the proposals; the more comparable the proposals, the more informative the analysis—and the easier the decision at the end of the process. Success therefore depends on meticulous, detailed preparation.

Preparation: First, familiarize yourself with the local market: What law firms are available? What do their profiles look like? What level of quality can they provide? How do clients evaluate these firms? Which clients do these law firms already represent? Early involvement of local colleagues on site and their support is extremely important. Overarching global company standards need to be followed and support a uniform configuration of business relationships worldwide. It is important to understand what parts of these standards may not work in the local market. To understand what adaptations are required, you need the local expertise of your colleagues in the country. With their help, you can draw up a long list of law firms that may qualify for the RFP. You must also define the goal of the RFP. In our case, the goal was collaboration with a few selected partners in Japan across all corporate subsidiaries with optimized costs. For this purpose, we wanted to change the remuneration system from "hourly rates" to "unit pricing." In addition to information about the quality of the legal advice, benchmarks for the usual pricing structures and price levels of a country were useful indicators and played an important part in the RFP.

The RFP: Next, you send the RFP documentation to the selected firms. We learned that it is very helpful to describe how the documents are to be dealt with as well as determining the necessary document format: Not every Excel file or pdf document created in the U.S. or in Germany functions the same way in Japan. It may be advisable to prepare the documents in a way that increased controllability of the responses, via drop-down menus or by limiting the number of choices for certain areas. The more specific the question, the more likely the answer will provide the desired information.

Analysis: A well-designed RFP makes analyzing the answers easier and allows price comparisons. Some firms will be eliminated right away due to their violations of the RFP rules. Using a weighting system will lead to an overall result for the remaining firms. An analysis of individual service and pricing components will result in a ranking list. Based on this, you can draw up a shortlist—in our case, ten law firms remained.

Up to this point, the RFP process is identical to other legal RFP processes. This changes in the next step: the visit of the firms in Japan and an immersion in a different culture.

The personal visit: To further reduce the number of firms to those that are the best "fit," you may want to consider a personal visit. This means investing a lot of time and money. The advantage of an on-site visit is that it enables you to check different components that are important in the legal services provided: good preparation, quality standards, efficiency, awareness of problems, the ability to differentiate between important and unimportant issues, business orientation, clear strategies, recommendations for action and risk assessments, team spirit, and competence with international clientele.

During a personal visit you have the opportunity to meet the entire team that will be working for you later. Personal meetings are substantially more informative than information on paper alone. You can see for yourself whether all attorneys speak English, for example. You could find this out by inviting the law firms to visit you. However, visiting them on location gives you a glimpse behind the scene. How does the law firm work? What's the work atmosphere? You can see for yourself how the organization functions in practice. How open is the firm to new technologies? Do they use technology to increase their efficiency?

A firm that is well prepared gives clients the hope that they will be equally well prepared when they work on our matters. The visit offers both parties an opportunity to clarify open issues more easily and directly. It also helps avoid misunderstandings that may arise from written communications or communication by telephone or video conferencing. Law firms will also appreciate the seriousness of the selection efforts made by the client. This substantially increases the competitive pressure on the law firms and generally leads to better negotiation results.

A personal visit is worth the time, effort, and expenses if you don't know the local market very well and associated cost in this market is sufficiently relevant to your company. In our situation, the selection decision would certainly have been very different without a personal visit. You may ask yourself who you should you visit and how many law firms? Do you have to meet with all of the incumbents, even those whose quality you are already familiar with? We believe that you should include your incumbent firms in the RFP. In the best-case scenario, your choice will be confirmed. You may also get new insights into these firms and see them from a new perspective. In any case, including them ensures fair conditions for all participants in the RFP.

It is necessary to define a time frame in advance, as you will not manage to visit more than two law firms a day, particularly if you want to post-process one visit and prepare the next one between appointments. If the personal impression plays a significant role in the selection process, it is necessary to objectivize the fundamentally subjective judgment as much as possible. To ensure that the visiting teams are interdisciplinary and intercultural, work on a formal agenda. Conduct a predefined evaluation round after each visit, followed by a calibration round at the end.

For the most part, we met highly professional and motivated teams of attorneys who were very well prepared. We received clear answers and explanations as well as excellent RFP documentation. However, here are some impressions that we gleaned from our visits in Japan:

- In a country like Japan, dining together is an integral part of a business relationship and gifts are a standard form of common courtesy. That does not necessarily satisfy the compliance requirements of global companies. However, you can politely refuse all invitations using the justification of the "fair and impartial selection process." If you are supported by a local colleague, he will often be the best ambassador. Alternatively, include a statement in the RFP documents that the firms should refrain from gifts and invitations of all types to ensure a fair selection process.

- Take plenty of business cards with you: Even at appointments in which the law firms are represented by more than 20 staff members, courtesy requires you to give each and every one of them a business card.

- A questionnaire sent in advance in which the law firms have provided one profile including a photo per attorney before our appointment made it easier to deal with a large number of new faces in a short time.

- While one law firm was equipped with state-of-the-art communication technology, the tour at the next firm led through dusty paper files. In one case, we were given a friendly, professional reception, while others appeared amazed by us visitors—as if we had forgotten to announce our visit beforehand. Naturally, this left us with corresponding impressions.

- Firms that make a good impression answered our questions clearly and unambiguously, explained their strategies in an easily understandable fashion, and complied with specified agenda items and time frames. Firms that left less good impressions presented their firm by jointly leafing through the firm's image brochure. Some didn't have answers for what we considered simple questions, such as the reason for having the firm's headquarters in another city.

- To understand how firms dealt with conflicts of interest, we were told that the firm worked for various significant competitors, but conflicts were precluded. Why? Because they were simply precluded. For us, this was a difficult attitude towards a delicate issue. The next law firm saw a potential for conflicts of interest, but was able to communicate clear rules for handling such conflicts. That was professional and helpful.

- It was very revealing that several firms that had worked for us in the past were particularly ill-prepared. They seemed to have become too complacent. We rated this as a lack of appreciation for an existing client relationship. What a shame.

- Being prepared is better than low-balling on price. In other words: cheap is not always good. If someone gains points with attractive terms in their proposal, a disastrous performance during the visit will result in the exclusion of the law firm from the selection process.

- Sometimes it's the little things that make the difference, particular those that show that you have given thought to the client's challenges: For example, one firm provided us with a seating chart with the names of all the firm's representatives waiting for us. This was very attentive and an extremely helpful courtesy.

The decision: If you've meticulously worked through the "small things," the evaluation of the parameters quality, price, and visit—with corresponding weighting—will result in a ranking. From this ranking, select the first two, three, four or five law firms (whatever your selection target was). Then take a step back: Is this a group of law firms that can appropriately represent your company? Have all of the initially specified parameters been met? If this is not the case, you may want to consider an adaptation based on strategic considerations. Is so, you have selected a small, exclusive group of firms with which your company will collaborate in the future. Through your selection process, you have ensured that your quality standards have been met, transparency increased, pricing structures and levels optimized, local expertise optimally utilized, global standards established, and structures harmonized.

Is your selection journey over? Hardly. Without appropriate communication of the decision to all of the countries and organizations of the corporation involved, you will not be successful in the implementation of your decision. You should communicate the information in a timely and comprehensive manner within your organizational structures so that your approach to the selection is not only understood, but implemented on a sustained basis. The continuous performance evaluation of the relevant law firm is one of the most important aspects of post-processing.

Bidding to win: Before, during, and after the RFP process

Melania Wenstrup

Procurement today has greater stature, more influence, and a wider reach than ever before. Procurement professionals increasingly make key selection decisions both at the initial screening stage and at the final presentation. While they may not yet be able to award a contract or assignment to a party single handedly, they certainly can disqualify from or promote to the process any chosen party at the early stages. Here are five tips to improve your chance to win procurement-led RFPs:

- Understand procurement's reach and how they are perceived internally by spending time with them early on. This will influence how you work with procurement throughout the process.

- Focus your time, efforts, and resources to find out about procurement's objectives. Learn what their business goals are and how the business is changing for them. Explore what they believe to be the most pressing problems hindering them from achieving the success they seek. Arm them with the information they need to achieve these objectives.

- Keep procurement informed of your progress, as you would any other influential decision maker.

- Where you have to tactfully challenge the procurement process for access to the business, convey to them why and how the sought-after access will benefit their business and/or help procurement fulfill their objectives.

- Do not hesitate to decline to submit a bid where you have no existing relationship and no access to forge such a relationship and develop a proper understanding of the opportunity.

Before the RFP: Large-scale opportunities are usually signaled long before an RFP is made public. Surpass your competition prior to the RFP and treat procurement as you would any other key stakeholder in the decision process. Demonstrate and convey your added value to procurement by helping them define the real business requirements and influence the parameters of the specification beforehand. See procurement as your partner, not your adversary.

- Engage early on and often. Get to know the procurement team and understand procurement's stature within the organization: how influential will they be in the decision-making process?

- Recognize procurement as a separate stakeholder with different needs and start to influence those needs: influence the specifications or decision criteria. Get procurement to "desire" an element within your scope of available services that the competition would be unable or unwilling to provide. Have procurement formally include it as an evaluation criterion.

- Understand how procurement evaluates its supplier base and how this drives their purchasing strategies.

- Add procurement to your mailing lists for relevant publications and invite them to appropriate events.

- Demonstrate your understanding of their organizations' internal and external environment, e.g. through regulatory initiatives or industry themes.

- Arrange meetings to discuss developments in the business and projects that might be in the pipeline. Make sure your informal relationships are fresh, in case you are not allowed to contact those involved in the RFP when it arrives.

- Find out what procurement is trying to achieve through the RFP, which may not necessarily be the same as the business. Although cost will be important, they will have other key drivers. Ask questions so that you can demonstrate how your RFP will help them achieve their goals.

Possible driver	How you can help procurement achieve their objectives
Price reduction	Although it is too simplistic to say that procurement is all about driving down costs, you cannot ignore this aspect. Price is likely to come under intense scrutiny. You need to ensure that procurement compares like for like: • talk about fees early (as you would in any process) • understand the scope of work clearly • understand the target's perception of the work (of value or viewed as commodity)

Possible driver	How you can help procurement achieve their objectives
	• be more aware of pricing innovation and be explicit on the value of cost efficiency initiatives. Be prepared to either accept lower margins in exchange for other concessions or have the confidence to walk away and focus on opportunities with higher returns.
Value for money	Value is an often-used word in RFPs and not easily defined. Getting the right balance between price and quality is important. Ensure you understand how to articulate the value you offer: • discuss the idea of value with the target • articulate tangible examples of value you offer • offer a visit of your premises to get a feel for how the team works • quantify the economic benefits of your quality • express valuable offerings in terms of cost saving to the target.
Service quality	Allow procurement to benchmark your quality against other firms: • quantify the economic benefits of your quality. Convert this to what is meaningful to procurement • ensure your communication style fits with your target client • offer sample KPIs.
Risk management or mitigation	Where an RFP is driven by or has associated risks for the business: • offer a review of draft terms early on • consider an Umbrella Services Agreement to apply to all contracts between you and target client • offer procurement a direct link to your contracts team.
Technology	Where technology adoption is a driver for the client: • offer to give a demonstration of relevant technology platforms, e.g. a client portal • consider including specialists in the RFP process to help discuss technology adoption or the use of technology in your work.
'Hard' drivers	Understand procurement's hard drivers such as risk minimization, contributing to sustainable profit, growth, cost reduction etc. Think about how procurement can bank on the promises you made in your proposition: • quantify them and show when and how they will be achieved • offer a guarantee when the cost savings of a project are measured over years

Possible driver	How you can help procurement achieve their objectives
	• consider a 'prebate' offer: an upfront discount • identify any barriers to success and offer to cover the costs e.g. offering to meet the costs of disruption or transition • offer a fixed fee.
'Soft' drivers	Communicate to understand the client's requirements: • demonstrate your understanding of different cultures and industries where appropriate • think about cultural fit, shared values, diversity. • consider 'shared' Corporate Social Responsibility events.

When articulating your proposition, consider a 'better, simpler, more value' approach:

- **Better**—focus on quality. Get across a definitive and tangible feeling of your service. What improvements can you offer? When can procurement expect to see these improvements? How will they be able to measure it? Does it drive sustainability?

- **Simpler**—focus on simplifying the process and service management. Procurement looks to eradicate any unnecessary added services, so avoid sounding too 'salesy' or pushing additional services.

- **More value**—focus on pricing competitively. Do some benchmarking and know your walk-away price.

During the RFP: Procurement's primary aim is to ensure a level playing field among bidders. This has widespread implications for the level of access to and information shared with bidders. If dealt with incorrectly, this can have the effect of increasing the advantage for the competing incumbent. Here are some tips on how to engage more effectively with procurement during the RFP process:

- Get pitch teams to speak with procurement during the pitch process and at the presentation stage. Ensure they understand the value you can add and how your service is different.

- Ask 'what can I do to help procurement make an impact?' Be collaborative, understand procurement's challenges (not just that they need financial quantification), but help them with their internal issues.

- Put yourself in their position given the situation at hand. What would you like/dislike? What would you expect from suppliers?

- Uncover what they are ultimately trying to achieve and the challenges hindering them from realizing these goals.

Procurement influence	How to maximize your chances of success
Restricted access	When facing blocked access, you are prevented from fully understanding the drivers behind the overt requirement and unable to introduce business value. Recognize that the blocked access may benefit certain competitors, including those who exploit high-level executive relationships or have the benefit of incumbency. However, if you do not have access, you cannot sell, so try to create access. Make requests for additional information or meetings: • be tactfully audacious—create a strong case for having access and be clear about why you need it. An example on how to create access—"Based on previous experience, our success rate is near to zero if we do not have access. Therefore we cannot proceed unless we meet with client executives." • think more laterally about creating a 'break through' opportunity—network to get to the end user of your service. For example, do key decision makers sit on other boards where you have relationships? Do you have relationships with shared investment bankers, financial services providers etc.? • be prepared to walk away if access and information are denied and you do not hear a compelling reason for the target to change.

Procurement influence	How to maximize your chances of success
Sharing information to all bidders	Sharing information to all bidders is time efficient and transparent for procurement. Procurement is able to identify top bidders by the impressions they create at 'bidder conferences.' Think carefully about the questions you submit and the impression you are creating: • scrutinize the specifications and clarify any ambiguity before bidding • it is unlikely that there will be points awarded for asking questions which the target could reasonably have expected you to find the answers to on their website or in their annual report • ask only for information that will help you develop a compelling proposition • give them a reason to answer. If you are asking for a high level of detail, explain why it is important and what the target will get out of it, e.g. "So that we can plan your work efficiently and maximize time and cost savings for you, please provide …" • you may wish to 'hold back' on some of your questions if these would give away your strategy or differentiators to the competition
Prescriptive document	Maximize your chances of a high score: • answer every element of the question, even if you feel you have answered it in a previous question. Do NOT cross-refer to other answers. • if you have been asked to put your response in their template, use their template and do not change it in any way • provide evidence to back up what you are saying—this makes the evaluators feel less subjective when scoring (and more likely to get you a higher score). • mirror the target's language, but do not use jargon • pay attention to word limits (may include wording on diagrams).

Procurement influence	How to maximize your chances of success
Scoring matrices	You need to work hard to score well: • ask in advance for the selection criteria and weighting so you can review your responses • ask how the target will evaluate the response. Will one person be marking the whole response, or will different sections be given to different people, and if so which ones? This allows you to gauge how you should write your answers e.g. key messages may need to be repeated in different sections if there are different evaluators. • be aware that different areas may be marked in different ways. For example, technical questions may be marked 0-5 whereas more subjective criteria may be marked using a RAG (red, amber, green) report and then given a pass or fail. Use case studies, methodologies and proof of past experience to show you are able to do the work and help the evaluator justify a higher score.
eAuctions	Some firms adopt eAuctions as part of the process. eAuctions are often used if looking for a price differentiator, often leaving quality subject to interpretation. There is no leverage for uncertainty: to maximize your chances of success offer definitive and tangible service qualities.

After the RFP: Win or lose—the importance of staying in touch and using the specific RFP as the opportunity to start building long-term business relationships is key to a better position next time around. Seek feedback from procurement and ensure they believe themselves to be partners in the organization in terms of success. Most procurement teams are very willing to give feedback, recognizing this as a way of improving the quality of future RFPs.

Anything you can glean from the scoring process and any peripheral elements of the decision can help you pitch more effectively next time. Continue to cultivate relationships with influential procurement teams and ensure they receive invitations to knowledge sharing events, relevant publications, newsletters, and any trends and issues that are critical to their success.

Successful legal sourcing

Jason Winmill

A few years ago, a conference on collaboration between sourcing professionals and their legal department colleagues was held in New York City. On stage, a sourcing executive (joined by his legal counterpart) from a leading pharmaceutical company was sharing his successful experience working with legal—and saving tens of millions of dollars. Some conference participants became uneasy and responded to the speaker: "At our company, legal matters move on tight timeline— typically days. We would never have the time to involve non-attorneys in our hiring process." "Our legal department has good long-standing relationships with our outside counsel; this ensures the best outcome. Our organization is satisfied that there is no better way." On display were two very different worldviews: on stage, evidence of a strategic partnership, sourcing and legal working together on tough issues. In the audience, for some, even the possibility of in-depth collaboration was anxiety-inducing. Our experience suggests that Corporate America is split into three distinct segments when it comes to sourcing and legal:

- The first segment is comprised of companies who are pioneering legal sourcing and continuing to improve and develop the space. This is the smallest segment. They are companies with very high legal spend; legal costs have become an important "pain point" for executive management outside of the legal department: Pfizer, Ebay, Caterpillar, JPMorgan Chase, Medtronic, Home Depot, and others. Legal departments who are recognized as leaders in these types of efficiency initiatives report that their efforts are ongoing. They stay "on it", refine, improve, and build on prior successes. For the most successful organizations, it's a multi-year journey and the best are never satisfied.

- The second group is companies who can only see reasons why sourcing and legal collaboration is impossible. We believe this is the largest segment of Fortune 500 companies. Lack of resources and the assertion that legal is "low on the priority list" are often cited by sourcing professionals as primary impediments to making progress. However, the real obstacles are a lack of expertise, non-robust working relationships with senior legal leaders (even though they might collaborate well on day-to-day contract review and management and other tactical issues), and lack of a viable strategic vision and proven tools tailored to the legal marketplace.

- The third group is positioned between these two groups. It is starting to target legal sourcing and making progress in selective and narrow ways. Although they lack a comprehensive and strategic approach, this group is gaining modest traction while gaining valuable skills and experience in limited, focused areas.

While Corporate America is making progress in legal sourcing, there is wide heterogeneity in approaches, skills, focus, scope, impact, and ultimately results. To continue to reap increased savings, legal sourcing professionals need to use thoughtful planning, build on their initial collaborations and have a more coordinated and sophisticated approach to managing the legal category for value, and be aware of possible issues:

RFPs are no panacea: RFPs have become a very popular tool for sourcing legal services as the volume and scope of RFPs show. Unless they are done correctly, however, RFPs may do more harm than good: Sourcing professionals who rely on traditional RFP models and approaches typically fall short in achieving a significant level of sustainable savings. Most of the RFPs we see issued to outside counsel are not properly designed nor customized to the unique aspects of the legal marketplace. They don't ask the right questions that lead to "decision-grade" data, and amount to little more than a "paper pushing" exercise that wastes the time of both outside counsel and in-house counsel. RFP programs launched without first developing a strategy can derail the entire process and backfire, with irreparable damage to the legal department's credibility with outside law firms.

Legal technology "mirage": Legal technology companies have talented sales forces and big marketing budgets. When legal cost management is considered, it is not surprising that the search often starts with a technology review. Legal technology has advanced over the past decade. It is more sophisticated and enhanced than ever. However, legal technology is never the "silver bullet." Legal technology solutions and applications can augment better decision making for attorneys, but those waiting for a technology-lead solution will be waiting for some time. We don't yet have the perfect systems to help manage law firms and provide true cost management as opposed to simply invoice management and high-level, directional cost guidance.

Law firms striking back: As sourcing advances, law firms are making adjustments to their business models and approaches. They are developing "counter-measures" to protect and advance their economic self-interests. These responses increase the difficulty (and reduce transparency) for sourcing professionals working in this space.

Senior legal support required, but not enough: Sourcing professionals at Fortune 500 companies sometimes falsely assume that sponsorship at the GC-level means that a legal sourcing initiative will lead to success. This fails to recognize that power and purchasing selection is highly decentralized in many large legal departments. "Rank and file" attorneys can often easily derail sourcing initiatives if not bought in.

Legal services involve real risk: Sourcing needs to consider the inherent risk in the legal environment. Traditionally, in-house counsel careers are built on judicious and wise management of risk, rather than cost-savings achievements.

Legal services are highly sophisticated: Sourcing professionals building credibility in the legal department are often faced with the challenge of moving along a steep learning curve while facing short-term savings expectations. Taking shortcuts (such as not understanding key legal concepts or proceeding without robust benchmarking data) is a common mistake—one that often jeopardizes legal sourcing initiatives.

An extremely fragmented legal marketplace: Sourcing professionals are used to dealing with national service providers or regional/local providers whose offerings are somewhat similar to national providers, making market comparisons possible. The number of law firms in the U.S. alone is between 45,000 and 50,000—a daunting set of market-data to analyze and manage.

Lawyers' mindset: Attorneys' typically vigorously defend their rights to autonomy and individualism, well beyond what is common in other professions. Some say they are trained and hired to be pessimistic and spot flaws. This professional outlook might be desirable when facing opposing counsel in a "must win" legal confrontation. However, it can make collaboration with other groups inside the corporation challenging.

Despite these issues, sourcing can make progress in the legal category with a thoughtful, careful, and strategic approach and appropriate dedicated resources. To achieve the highest levels of legal sourcing success, sourcing professional should consider:

Have legal make decisions, but help navigate: Most successful sourcing initiatives are "attorney-led." Sourcing can be effective when it:
- Provides high-quality benchmarking data that highlights current gaps and potential opportunities
- Sketches realistic, specific strategic options for legal to pursue
- Outlines tested "best practices" for legal to consider
- Provides ongoing value-added support for new enhanced processes

Provide legal with proven, viable options: Offering in-house counsel options—rather than lobbying for a single approach—ensures that legal stays in the driver's seat and increase their level of comfort.

Manage legal costs on multiple fronts: Most legal sourcing initiatives improve legal cost performance by managing multiple "levers." Reliance on any one lever is likely to be disappointing, limited, and may leave significant money on the table. The strategic sourcing initiative at a major energy company involved four levers:
- Improved firm selection
- More active management of billing rates
- Rationalization of staffing mix, and
- Implementation of AFAs

Data and reliable information are critical inputs for sourcing: Market intelligence, pricing data, and meaningful benchmarks are contributions that procurement can offer. Sourcing can help by bringing robust benchmarking data to the table that shows meaningful comparisons across relevant peer companies by performing "landscape scans" to identify non-traditional vendors, billing models, and other opportunities on the horizon.

Work with legal's deadlines, not sourcing's: Legal departments frequently have non-negotiable deadlines. Some skeptical in-house attorneys hold the notion that sourcing could cause legal to miss these deadlines and therefore jeopardize the outcome of critical legal matters. It is important not to validate these misconceptions.

Find allies in unlikely places: Pricing directors and other business managers in law firms can be potential allies for sourcing. Though these professionals may be attorneys, they tend to be less involved in case strategy and more involved in improving case management and the health of the overall relationship with clients.

About the authors

Catherine Alman MacDonagh

CEO & Founder, Legal Lean Sigma Institute
Boston, MA
www.legalleansigma.com
Twitter: @CathMacDonagh
linkedin.com/pub/catherine-alman-macdonagh-jd/2/a29/35b

Dr. George Beaton

Executive Chairman, Beaton Research + Consulting
Melbourne (Australia)
www.beatonglobal.com
Twitter: @grbeaton_law
au.linkedin.com/in/georgerbeaton

Toby Brown

Chief Practice Officer, Akin Gump Strauss Hauer & Feld LLP
Houston, TX
www.akingump.com
Twitter: @gnawledge
linkedin.com/in/tobinbrown

Richard Burcher

Managing Director & Pricing Consultant, Validatum
London (UK)
www.validatum.com
Twitter: @validatum
uk.linkedin.com/in/validatum

Eric Chin

Senior Analyst, Beaton Research + Consulting
Melbourne (Australia)
www.beatonglobal.com
Twitter: @ericjychin
au.linkedin.com/pub/eric-chin/17/190/60

David Clark

Head of Bid Management, APS Group
Manchester (UK)
www.theapsgroup.com
Twitter: @thebidbod
uk.linkedin.com/pub/david-clark/4/96/438

Timothy B. Corcoran

Principal, Corcoran Consulting Group LLC
Lawrenceville, NJ
www.corcoranlawbizblog.com
Twitter: @tcorcoran
linkedin.com/in/tcorcoran

Vincent Cordo, Jr.

Global Director Client Value, Reed Smith LLP
Pittsburgh, PA
www.reedsmith.com
Twitter: @vcordo
linkedin.com/in/vincentcordo

John de Forte

Owner, Proposal Training Ltd. and de Forte Associates
London (UK)
www.deforte.com
uk.linkedin.com/pub/john-de-forte/7/292/838

Danny Ertel

Partner/Founder, Vantage Partners LLC
Boston, MA
www.vantagepartners.com
Twitter: @DannyErtel
linkedin.com/pub/danny-ertel/0/978/5b1

Geraint Evans

Head of New Business, CMS Cameron McKenna
London (UK)
www.cms-cmck.com
uk.linkedin.com/in/geraintevans1

D. Casey Flaherty

Corporate Counsel, Kia Motors
Los Angeles, CA
www.kia.com www.legaltechaudit.com
Twitter: @dcaseyflaherty
linkedin.com/pub/d-casey-flaherty/22/124/491

Arne Gärtner

Research Assistant, Bucerius Center on the Legal Profession
Hamburg (Germany)
www.bucerius-clp.de
de.linkedin.com/pub/arne-gärtner/46/605/a26/en

Charles H. Green

CEO/Founder, Trusted Advisor Associates
West Orange, NJ
www.trustedadvisor.com
Twitter: @charleshgreen
linkedin.com/in/charleshgreen

Markus Hartung

Director, Bucerius Center on the Legal Profession
Berlin (Germany)
www.bucerius-clp.de
Twitter: @mchartung
de.linkedin.com/pub/markus-hartung/9/44b/1a

Dr. Silvia Hodges Silverstein

Executive Director, Buying Legal Council
New York, NY
www.buyinglegal.com
Twitter: @buyinglegal @silviahodges
linkedin.com/in/silviahodges

Lynn D. Krauss

Assistant General Counsel & Chief of Staff, Dow Corning
Saginaw, MI
www.dowcorning.com
linkedin.com/pub/lynn-krauss/21/437/9b1

Andy Krebs

Global Strategic Sourcing Manager, Intel Corporation
Phoenix, AZ
www.intel.com
linkedin.com/pub/andy-krebs/4/904/a76

Brian Lee

Managing Director, CEB Legal Leadership Council, CEB
Washington, DC
www.executiveboard.com
linkedin.com/in/blee25

Steven Manton

Strategic Pricing Leader, Debevoise & Plimpton LLP
New York, NY
www.debevoise.com
linkedin.com/pub/steven-manton/b/598/657

Colleen F. Nihill

Chief Administrative Officer, Dechert LLP
Philadelphia, PA
www.dechert.com
linkedin.com/pub/colleen-nihill/3/550/9a

Susan O'Brien

Principal & Founder, Sourcing Logics LLC
Brookfield, CT
www.sourcinglogics.com
Twitter: @SourcingLogics
linkedin.com/pub/susan-o-brien/1/b73/78

Daria Radchenko

Senior Project Manager, Beaton Research + Consulting
Melbourne (Australia)
www.beatonglobal.com
au.linkedin.com/pub/daria-radchenko/51/59b/196

Dr. Ute Rajathurai

Head of Global Legal Spend Management, Bayer Business Services
Leverkusen (Germany)
www.bayer.com
linkedin.com/pub/ute-rajathurai/61/610/5a2

Melania Wenstrup

National Business Development and Marketing Manager, BDO LLP
London (UK)
www.bdo.com
Twitter: @MelaniaWenstrup
linkedin.com/profile/view?id=11409374&trk=tyah2&locale=en_US

Jason Winmill

Managing Partner, Argopoint
Boston, MA
www.argopoint.com
linkedin.com/pub/jason-winmill/2/69b/717

Bill Young

Management Consultant, PA Consulting
Basel (Switzerland)
www.paconsulting.com
Twitter: @billkestrel
linkedin.com/pub/bill-young/0/19b/224

63694802R00120

Made in the USA
Lexington, KY
15 May 2017